AMERICAN EXPANSION
IN THE LATE NINETEENTH CENTURY

With the Compliments of
**KRIEGER
PUBLISHING COMPANY**
Malabar, FL

AMERICAN EXPANSION IN THE LATE NINETEENTH CENTURY

Colonialist or Anticolonialist?

Edited by **J. ROGERS HOLLINGSWORTH**
University of Wisconsin

ROBERT E. KRIEGER PUBLISHING COMPANY
MALABAR, FLORIDA
1983

Original Edition 1968
Reprint Edition 1983

Printed and Published by
ROBERT E. KRIEGER PUBLISHING COMPANY, INC.
KRIEGER DRIVE
MALABAR, FL 32950

Printed in the United States of America

Library of Congress Cataloging in Publication Data

Main entry under title:
American expansion in the late nineteenth century.
  colonialist or anticolonialist?

  Reprint. Originally published: New York:
Holt, Rinehart, and Winston, 1968.
    1. United States—Foreign relations—1865-1898—
Addresses, essays, lectures. 2. United States—
Territorial expansions—Addresses, essays, lectures.
I. Hollingsworth, J. Rogers (Joseph Rogers), 1932-
E661.7.A53 1983   327.73   82-10008
ISBN 0-89874-531-4   AACR2

CONTENTS

Introduction   1

THE INTELLECTUAL ROOTS OF AMERICAN EXPANSION

JULIUS W. PRATT—The Ideology of American Expansionism   9
CHARLES VEVIER—American Continentalism   18

DEPRESSION AND EXPANSION

RICHARD HOFSTADTER—Depression and Psychic Crisis   25
NELSON M. BLAKE—Reaffirmation of the Monroe Doctrine   29
WALTER LaFEBER—The Need for Foreign Markets   41

THE ORIGINS OF THE SPANISH-AMERICAN WAR

JULIUS W. PRATT—The Business Point of View   51
WALTER LaFEBER—McKinley, the Business Community,
  and Cuba   59

POLITICAL GOALS OF THE SPANISH-AMERICAN WAR

LOUIS J. HALLE—Drifting War Policies   68
ROBERT E. OSGOOD—Ideals and Self-interest in Foreign Policy   76
CHRISTOPHER LASCH—The Anti-imperialists and the Inequality
  of Man   89

THE OPEN DOOR POLICY: ROUTE TO AMERICAN EXPANSION

WILLIAM A. WILLIAMS—Imperial Anticolonialism   96
CHARLES S. CAMPBELL, JR.—The Role of Business Interests   100
GEORGE F. KENNAN—An Inadequate Policy   109

SUGGESTIONS FOR FURTHER READING   118

$50,000 REWARD.—WHO DESTROYED THE MAINE?—$50,000 REWARD

NEW YORK JOURNAL
AND ADVERTISER.   FIRST EDITION.

The Journal will give $50,000 for information, furnished to it exclusively, that will convict the person or persons who sank the Maine.

The Journal will give $50,000 for information, furnished to it exclusively, that will convict the person or persons who sank the Maine.

NO. 5,372.   Copyright, 1898, by W. R. Hearst.—NEW YORK, THURSDAY, FEBRUARY 17, 1898.—16 PAGES.   PRICE ONE CENT

DESTRUCTION OF THE WAR SHIP MAINE WAS THE WORK OF AN ENEMY

$50,000!

$50,000 REWARD!
For the Detection of the Perpetrator of the Maine Outrage!

The New York Journal to-day offers of $50,000 CASH for the FURNISHED TO IT EXCLUSIVELY, which shall lead to the detection and conviction of the person or persons criminally responsible for the explosion which resulted in the destruction, at Havana, of the United States war ship Maine and the loss of 253 lives of American sailors.

The $50,000 CASH offered for the above information to be on deposit with Wells, Fargo & Co. and will be paid upon the production of the convincing evidence.

No one believes the Spanish Government will give up the guilty officials responsible for the explosion—a few honorable dollars to bring to a court or bar of a government criminally responsible for the plotting by our destined means to avenge the cruel insult to crippled American sailors.

This offer has been asked to Europe and will be made public by cable at the Continent and in London this morning.

The Journal believes that the men who set the bomb had accomplices. FOR THE PERPETRATOR OF THIS OUTRAGE HAD ACCOMPLICES.
W. R. Hearst.

Assistant Secretary Roosevelt Convinced the Explosion of the War Ship Was Not an Accident.

The Journal Offers $50,000 Reward for the Conviction of the Criminals Who Sent 258 American Sailors to Their Death.
Naval Officers Unanimous That the Ship Was Destroyed on Purpose.

$50,000!

$50,000 REWARD!
For the Detection of the Perpetrator of the Maine Outrage!

The New York Journal to-day offers a reward of $50,000 CASH for information FURNISHED TO IT EXCLUSIVELY, which shall lead to the detection and conviction of the person or persons criminally responsible for the explosion which resulted in the destruction, at Havana, of the United States war ship Maine and the loss of 253 lives of American sailors.

The $50,000 CASH offered for the above information to be on deposit with Wells, Fargo & Co. and will be paid upon the production of the convincing evidence.

No one believes the Spanish Government will give up the guilty officials responsible for the explosion—a few honorable dollars to bring to a court or bar of a government criminally responsible for the plotting by our destined means to avenge the cruel insult to crippled American sailors.

This offer has been asked to Europe and will be made public by cable at the Continent and in London this morning.

The Journal believes that the men who set the bomb had accomplices. FOR THE PERPETRATOR OF THIS OUTRAGE HAD ACCOMPLICES.
W. R. Hearst.

POWDER MAGAZINE

NAVAL OFFICERS THINK THE MAINE WAS DESTROYED BY A SPANISH MINE.

George Eugene Bryson, the Journal's special correspondent at Havana, cables that it is the secret opinion of many Spaniards in the Cuban capital, that the Maine was destroyed and 258 of her men killed by means of a submarine mine, or fixed torpedo. This is the opinion of several American naval authorities. The Spaniards, it is believed, arranged to have the Maine anchored over one of the harbor mines. Mines connected the mine with a powder magazine, and it is thought the explosion was caused by sending an electric current through this wire. If this can be proven, the brutal nature of the Spaniards will be shown by the fact that they waited to spring the mine until after all the men had retired for the night. The Maine's consort in picture down where it is believed to have been the mine.

Hidden Mine or a Sunken Torpedo Believed to Have Been the Weapon Used Against the American Man-of-War---Officers and Men Tell Thrilling Stories of Being Blown Into the Air Amid a Mass of Shattered Steel and Exploding Shells---Survivors Brought to Key West Scout the Idea of Accident---Spanish Officials Protest Too Much---Our Cabinet Orders a Searching Inquiry---Journal Sends Divers to Havana to Report Upon the Condition of the Wreck.
Was the Vessel Anchored Over a Mine?

Assistant Secretary of the Navy Theodore Roosevelt says he is convinced that the destruction of the Maine in Havana Harbor was not an accident. The Journal offers a reward of $50,000 for exclusive evidence that will convict the person, persons or Government criminally responsible for the destruction of the American battleship and the death of 258 of its crew.

The suspicion that the Maine was deliberately blown up grows stronger every hour. Not a single fact to the contrary has been produced.

Captain Sigsbee, of the Maine, and Consul-General Lee both urge that public opinion be suspended until they have completed their investigation. They are taking the course of tactful men who are convinced that there has been treachery.

Spanish Government officials are pressing forward all sorts of explanations of how it could have been an accident. The facts show that there was a report before the ship exploded, and that, had her magazine exploded, she would have sunk immediately.

Every naval expert in Washington says that if the Maine's magazine had exploded the whole vessel would have been blown to atoms.

The sinking of the *Maine*, as featured in Hearst's *New York Journal* on February 17, 1898. (*The Granger Collection*)

INTRODUCTION

Diplomatic historians have long viewed 1898 as a turning point in American history. Certainly the events associated with the Spanish-American War provided the nation with commitments and responsibilities unlike any it had ever faced. Clearly, the war made governments everywhere realize that the United States had attained the status of a great power.

Having emphasized the distinctive features of the Spanish-American War and its consequences for American diplomacy, historians are now concerned with the historical context out of which war emerged. Viewed in this perspective, the events of 1898 and 1899 are part of a long tradition of American expansion and do not mark a sharp break with the past.

Present-day historians are particularly preoccupied with emphasizing expansionism as one of the most important forces in American history. This focus on expansionism is quite understandable, given the fact that never before in all human history had one nation grown in less than four hundred years from a series of small settlements to a country with a population of almost two hundred million people and military bases on every continent. One of the most important problems in American history is to understand why and how such a rapid rate of expansion occurred.

The nature of American expansion during the late nineteenth century is discussed from different points of view in the following essays. They focus on the extent to which the nation's expansionist policies were carefully directed by high-level policy makers, were the result of drift and inertia among policy makers, or were the result of a widely shared sense of mission or destiny which was deeply ingrained in the American tradition.

There has long been a debate over the extent to which overseas expansion was deliberately calculated by those who were charged with making public policy. The authors of several of the following essays disagree over the extent to which expansionist policies were managed by events or men. One view suggests that policy makers clearly knew what they wanted and were successful in moving the nation in the desired direction. Another view suggests that American foreign policy during the late nineteenth century was so democratic and pluralistic in its impulses that no one was capable of governing. Indeed, it is often so difficult to find the time and place when decisions were made that it becomes easy to characterize American expansion as a product of governmental action which was simply drifting out of control.

1

If the student is to understand American expansion, he obviously must focus on phenomena other than decision making. He should assess the extent to which expansion stemmed from such sources as the national character of the American people, the extent to which the American people believed it was their destiny, their mission, to carry out certain kinds of expansion. To deal with these problems, he must first understand the broad cultural context within which expansionism occurred. Fortunately, Julius W. Pratt and Charles Vevier have attempted to delineate certain features of the intellectual framework within which American expansion took place.

In the first essay presented here, Pratt does not endeavor to explain why American expansion occurred. He attempts to analyze the pietistic justification Americans have offered from time to time in defense of their particular brand of expansionism. His essay is not, strictly speaking, diplomatic history; rather, it deals with the "inner springs" of diplomatic history. His study rests on the premise that public policy in a democratic society is shaped by values which are shared throughout the nation, that to analyze the decisions of policy makers about American expansion, it is necessary to understand the nation's value system. And Pratt has made a useful contribution by demonstrating the relationship between the nation's cultural tradition and the justification offered by articulate Americans in defense of their expansionist activities.

Like Pratt, Vevier is concerned with the relationship between popular ideology and public policy. But Vevier examines the problem from the perspective of American arguments in support of a "continentalist" policy. Desiring the territorial expansion that resulted in the acquisition of contiguous territory in North America, the American people had domesticated their foreign policy. Unlike most European countries in which foreign and domestic policies constituted two distinct spheres of action, the United States had domestic and foreign policies that were intricately linked. Numerous Americans believed that expansion of the nation's commerce over the entire world was needed to assist in the development of the American continent. In other words, world commercial expansion and American territorial expansion were viewed as necessary to each other. Vevier contends that these ideas had a long tradition in American history and that they had a significant impact on American thinking during the 1890s.

Vevier does not entirely disagree with Pratt's implication that Americans saw expansion as the unfolding of God's will, as part of their destiny. Indeed, he suggests that a few people saw in expansion the development of American destiny. But according to him, this was not the case with most American continentalists. Most expansionists believed they had considerable freedom of action, and they attempted to make expansionist decisions in geopolitical terms.

There is a somewhat unclear relationship between American foreign policy and the ideas Pratt and Vevier have delineated. What was the real relationship between public policy and widely disseminated ideas about expansion? Did American policy makers actually support certain kinds of expansion because they believed their destiny was involved? Did policy makers support American commercial expansion as a means of strengthening American continentalism?

Implicitly, both Pratt and Vevier assume that foreign policy was influenced by the attitudes which an intellectual elite espoused. Because the interaction between popular ideas and government policies is exceedingly difficult to study, many questions remain unanswered. Should Pratt and Vevier assume that policy makers were responding to certain ideas simply because those ideas were popular at the time? What evidence is there that policy makers were actually aware of certain popular views of the day? When different people advocated similar ideas at two separtate points in history, should the historian attribute some kind of intellectual kinship to them? In other words, what kind of evidence is necessary to demonstrate the influence of expansionists of the 1850s and 1860s on exponents of expansion of the 1890s?

These are only a few of the problems involved in studying the relationship between public opinion and public policy. Yet most studies of American expansion are filled with implications bearing on these questions, frequently leading historians either to view foreign policy as shaped by pressure groups advocating highly rational means to promote the goals of governmental policy or to see foreign policy as drifting out of control because of the influence of an uninformed public pursuing parochial or misguided policies. Because we have a number of case studies bearing on late-nineteenth-century American expansion, it is possible to study in some detail specific expansionist policies. The Venezuelan boundary dispute provides an excellent opportunity to study American expansion, for most of the attitudes, pressures, and premises that shaped the nation's expansionist policies during the 1890s were present. It is also useful to study the Venezuelan boundary dispute for purposes of comparing it with other episodes in American expansion. It will be especially interesting for the student not only to compare the outcome of the Venezuelan and Cuban situations but also to contrast the involvement of public and private interest groups in the two episodes.

Why did the United States react to the Venezuelan boundary dispute as it did? Clearly, Richard Hofstadter does not view the government's policy as one that was carefully planned by public officials. Rather, he argues that a long tradition of anti-English sentiment, combined with frustrations generated by an acute economic depression, produced a kind of national psychosis which was extremely belligerent in tone. It was to this belligerent spirit that the Cleveland Administration was responding when it took the nation to the brink of war.

But Hofstadter is not clear as to why President Cleveland reacted to rampant jingoism in such vigorous terms. Had the President also become caught up in the psychic crisis of the 1890s? Was he simply drifting with the tide of public sentiment? If so, how does one reconcile such an explanation with the widely held view that Cleveland was inflexible and courageous in not responding to public opinion on most issues of the day? While a close analysis of Hofstadter's essay raises these questions, they are not answered.

Nelson M. Blake contends that the seriousness with which the Administration took the Venezuelan boundary crisis was due to the public agitation over the matter. In contrast to Hofstadter, Blake portrays the government as acting quite rationally. He argues that Cleveland, in addition to responding to the public clamor, was convinced that the Monroe Doctrine was being challenged and that it was his duty to defend it.

Assuming that Cleveland was acting much more responsibly than Hofstadter implies, Blake still does not explain why Cleveland believed the Monroe Doctrine was worth upholding at the risk of war. This, Walter LaFeber attempts to do, by suggesting that Cleveland's diplomacy was influenced by domestic economic considerations. Unlike Hofstadter, LaFeber views the policy as a rational and serious effort to face some of the nation's most acute economic problems. He argues that the Cleveland Administration believed that the health of the economy would improve only when foreign markets were found for the nation's expanding productivity. Cleveland was especially interested in Latin America as a region for economic expansion, but Great Britain appeared to pose a threat to this country's long-range plans in the area. According to LaFeber, Cleveland used the Venezuelan boundary dispute as a means of halting the spread of Britain's influence there and as an instrument for informing the world of the importance of Latin America to the United States.

Though it is generally agreed that the search for foreign markets was an important factor in shaping American foreign policy during the 1890s, there is considerable diversity in the assessment of the relationship between economic factors and American expansion. This is especially the case with the problems pertaining to the Spanish-American War. Even so, nearly every historian of the Spanish-American War attempts to answer one basic question: was the United States drawn into the war by businessmen in search of raw materials and markets for manufactured goods, as Marxist historians have suggested? Julius W. Pratt answers no. He points out that American businessmen were in search of foreign markets, but he argues that, with the exception of the business interests which were tied directly to the Cuban sugar market, the financial and business sectors of the country opposed war and were not of any consequence in promoting it.

Because President McKinley has usually been portrayed as a pawn of American business interests, one immediately asks why he eventually recommended a policy that carried the nation to war if the business community was so firmly opposed to war. Does this suggest that McKinley was substantially more independent of the business community than we are usually led to believe? Or is it possible that business attitudes toward war were somewhat different from those which Pratt found? Or could the nation have drifted into war despite the opposition of both the business community and McKinley?

Because McKinley first attempted to follow a neutralist policy in Cuba, historians have long attempted to pinpoint the group that finally forced the McKinley Administration to abandon its resistance to war. As a result, publishers such as

William Randolph Hearst and Joseph Pulitzer, expansionists Alfred Thayer Mahan, Henry Cabot Lodge, and Theodore Roosevelt, and even spokesmen for American Protestantism have been blamed for stirring up war sentiment. Meanwhile, McKinley has been protrayed as a spineless uninformed president who permitted the nation to drift into war by surrendering to various belligerent groups.

Recently, McKinley has appeared in a more favorable light. Walter LaFeber has argued that McKinley held tight reins over governmental policy during the spring of 1898 and that the government's policy was carefully designed to protect the nation's vital interests. LaFeber describes McKinley's policies prior to the spring of 1898 as being dedicated to obtaining autonomy for the Cubans within the Spanish empire. When the Spanish finally were prepared to grant such a request, the Cuban rebels were no longer willing to settle for less than independence.

LaFeber argues that McKinley's policies changed at that point. This occurred, in part, because various business groups were influential in convincing the President that unless independence were granted to the Cubans, the fighting would continue and would eventually permit a group of Cuban radicals to assume power. In the opinion of LaFeber, McKinley believed that this would have unsettling effects on the American economy. Though LaFeber disagrees with Pratt concerning the role businessmen played in shaping McKinley's war plans, he certainly makes no suggestion that businessmen were involved in anything resembling a conspiracy. Rather, he contends that McKinley became so convinced that the economic interests of the United States were intricately tied to a policy of Cuban pacification that he was willing to take the steps leading to such an end even if war were the result.

Unfortunately, there are no historical sources that can reveal definitively why McKinley acted as he did in the spring of 1898. Historians will probably continue to be divided between those who believe he coolly and deliberately attempted to carry out a Cuban policy to protect the nation's vital interests and those who believe he drifted into war as a result of manipulation by jingoists acting from selfish and irresponsible motives.

It is also difficult to explain how the Cuban situation eventually made the United States a world power with commitments halfway around the globe. Was a widely shared sense of destiny at work? Or a kind of uncontrolled drift? Or did the United States acquire an empire on the basis of carefully chosen policies?

Pratt argues that most spokesmen for the Protestant and business communities were opposed to war in the spring of 1898 but that once hostilities occurred they helped to promote such fruits of war as the annexation of Hawaii, Guam, and the Philippines. But what was the impact of these groups on McKinley? Did he develop his war plans somewhat independently of domestic pressures, with the realization that his conduct of the war would eventually commit the United States to an empire?

Louis J. Halle suggests that events drifted somewhat out of control, that the Administration had no plans before or during the war for acquiring an Asian empire. While no one has suggested that McKinley went to war with plans to annex the Philippines, Halle contends that the decision to occupy the Philippines was not made until after they were attached to the United States. In essence, Halle argues that McKinley was not the maker of policy; rather, his function was to provide a stamp of legitimacy on events that were leading the Administration.

Though considerable sentiment developed for retention of the Philippines following victory in the Bay of Manila, there was in this country a polarization of opinion on the subject as debate raged between imperialists and anti-imperialists. Because he believes that domestic attitudes played an important role in shaping the nation's expansionism, Robert E. Osgood attempted to study American foreign policy by focusing on both groups. He concluded that the decisions which shaped American foreign policy during this period were usually irrational, impulsive, unstable, and ineffective. For Osgood, this was so because decision makers were heavily influenced by the force of tradition and by values which were deeply ingrained in the American system but which had little relevance to the realities of international politics. The net result, according to Osgood, was the failure of the United States to make a mature adjustment to its international environment.

But what would a mature adjustment have been? Osgood is not entirely successful in spelling this out, though he argues convincingly that the United States could not have a far-ranging empire and yet remain attached intellectually to policies of geographical isolationism and high idealism. Despite the idealism inherent in the thinking of both the imperialists and the anti-imperialists, neither, according to Osgood, had an adequate understanding of what should be the proper relationship between means and goals of American foreign policy.

For some groups, this failure resulted because their thinking about foreign policy was dictated by domestic considerations that were often quite parochial in nature. Whereas the anti-imperialists are usually portrayed as being motivated by idealistic and humanitarian considerations, Christopher Lasch demonstrates that many anti-imperialists shared a pseudo-Darwinian approach to politics. Numerous Southerners denounced an imperialist policy not because of any strategic concern with the country's relations with other nations but because they were opposed to permitting more "colored" people to enter the body politic.

But it would be a mistake to assume that all imperialists and anti-imperialists were without an adequate understanding of the country's role in the community of nations. When one focuses on some of the common concerns of the imperialists and anti-imperialists, it becomes apparent that many in both groups were engaged in a serious dialogue about American foreign policy. William A. Williams points out that the imperialists and anti-imperialists were in agreement that overseas economic expansion was necessary for the nation's economic well-being. Their chief differences were over the means to be employed to achieve it. The imperialists believed formal colonization and governmental control to be necessary, while most anti-imperialists thought economic expansion could be achieved without the expense of a colonial empire.

Though the imperialists appear to have won the debate, Williams suggests that the views of the anti-imperialists were eventually incorporated into the Open Door policy, which in essence became the cornerstone of American foreign policy. The Open Door policy, according to Williams, provided a temporary settlement of the issue of imperialism in the United States, and it represented a realistic effort to gain the benefits of economic expansion without the expense of an empire.

The reader should note that certain aspects of the Open Door policy were not novel with the McKinley Administration but represented a new way of demanding the commercial rights of the "most-favored-nation" policy, an important ingredient of American foreign policy since 1776. By the "most-favored-nation" policy, the United States was assured that it would enjoy the same trade relations with a state as the most privileged nation enjoyed in trade relations with that state. In other words, tradition played an important role in shaping the Open Door policy. The Open Door notes did, however, go beyond the "most-favored-nation" principle. One need look only at the provision concerning the territorial integrity of China to realize that the notes were not simply a reaffirmation of the "most-favored-nation" principle. On the other hand, the Administration could have gone further than it did, for John Hay had called for an open door for trade but not for investment.

Like most foreign policy decisions, a variety of domestic forces were responsible for the Open Door policy. This, Charles S. Campbell, Jr. demonstrates with a case study on pressure politics. He points out that the *Journal of Commerce* and the Asiatic Association pressured the Administration into becoming aware of the importance of protecting American commercial rights in China. These pressure groups, and eventually the Adminstration as well, believed that if China were not carved into special spheres of interest, the United States would eventually be able to capture the largest share of Chinese markets. Equality of commercial opportunity was the carefully chosen instrument for promoting economic expansion in other parts of the world.

George F. Kennan views the Open Door policy with a perspective quite different from that of Williams and Campbell. The basis for disagreement revolves essentially around three questions: (1) What were the origins of the policy? (2) What was the Open Door designed to achieve in international politics? (3) What were its consequences, immediately and in the long run, on foreign as well as domestic politics? Instead of viewing the Open Door policy as a careful effort to extend the nation's economic influence in Asia, Kennan argues that the policy was shaped primarily by an Englishman, A. E. Hippisley, an employee of the Inspectorate of Maritime Customs in China. Kennan does not perceive the Open Door notes as part of a realistic and pragmatic effort to promote American economic expansion; rather, he sees the Open Door policy as prompted by an inadequate understanding of Asian politics. But regardless of whether the Open Door notes represented a realistic response to Western involvement in Asian affairs, subsequent administrations gave the notes an interpretation far beyond anything McKinley and Hay imagined at the time. Perhaps Kennan's attitude toward the Open Door policy is shaped more by his appraisal of what subsequent administrations permitted the policy to become than by an assessment of what it represented at the turn of the century.

To examine the process of expansionism in the late nineteenth century is indeed to open Pandora's box. Most studies have emphasized the public involvement in the decision-making process. Pratt analyzed expansion from the viewpoint of the participants and emphasized their sense of a shared destiny. Believing that destiny impelled the United States to world prominence, these participants viewed themselves more as being acted upon than as active, more as being influenced than influential.

The historian who assigns more credit to the public is not necessarily implying intelligent choices, however. Suggesting that the public generally had little understanding of international politics, Halle, Osgood, and Kennan agree that the public played an important role in shaping the government's expansionist policies. According to these authors, the public did not believe that what happened beyond the nation's borders posed much of a threat to its democratic institutions or territorial integrity; because of their legalistic and moralistic approach to international politics, Americans were anxious to impose their values on other parts of the world, whether the nation's security was involved or not. In this view, the nation's expansionist policies were shortsighted and inconsistent, more frequently than not, a product of drift.

LaFeber, Williams, and Campbell tend to suggest either that the public was relatively well informed as to what was in the national interest or the irrational sectors of the public exerted only a minimal influence on the government's expansionist policies. Somewhat in the tradition of Max Weber, these historians are inclined to view policy makers of a modern industrial society as involved in careful planning, usually attempting to relate well-chosen means to desired ends of policy. While these writers are concerned with the influence of domestic pressure groups on policy makers, their emphasis is placed on the influence of the rational, efficiency-oriented businessmen who attempted to use governmental power to enhance economic expansion abroad.

Until historians learn more about the process of decision making in a democratic society, they will be engaged in deciding if expansion was promoted by policy makers as a result of carefully calculated risks or if expansionism was usually the result of events and pressures over which presidential administrations exercised inadequate control.

In the reprinted selections footnotes appearing in the original sources have in general been omitted unless they contribute to the argument or better understanding of the selection.

JULIUS W. PRATT (1888-   ), professor emeritus of history at Buffalo University, is one of the most distinguished scholars of American expansionism. His published works include *Expansionists of 1812* and *Expansionists of 1898*. In most of his writing, Pratt has attempted to relate the ideological outlook of the American people to their expansionism. Using this approach, Pratt, in this essay, focuses on the justification the American people have offered for various kinds of expansionism. But why have the American people attempted to justify their expansionism in terms of divine sanction? And what impact did this particular kind of justification have on the nature of American expansionism?°

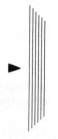

The Ideology of American Expansionism

Lincoln Steffens has observed that Americans have never learned to do wrong knowingly; that whenever they compromise with principle or abandon it, they invariably find a pious justification for their action. One is reminded of this observation in reviewing the history of American territorial expansion. For every step in that process, ingenious minds have found the best of reasons. From the year 1620, when King James the First granted to the Council for New England certain "large and goodlye Territoryes" in order "to second and followe God's sacred Will," to the year 1898, when William McKinley alleged that he had divine sanction for taking the Philippine Islands, it has been found possible to fit each successive acquisition of territory into the pattern of things decreed by divine will or inescapable destiny. The avowal of need or greed, coupled with power to take, has never satisfied our national conscience. We needed Florida and the mouth of the Mississippi; we thought we needed Canada, Texas, Oregon, California. But when we took, or attempted to take, that which we needed, we persuaded ourselves that we were but fulfilling the designs of Providence or the laws of Nature. If some of the apologists for later ventures in expansion were more frank in avowing motives of "national interest," the pious or fatalistic justification was none the less present.

°Reprinted from Julius W. Pratt, "The Ideology of American Expansion," in *Essays in Honor of William E. Dodd*, edited by Avery O. Craven (Chicago: The University of Chicago Press, 1935), pp. 335-353. Copyright 1935 by The University of Chicago. Reprinted by permission of the publisher. Footnotes omitted.

The idea of a destiny which presides over and guides American expansion has rarely, if ever, been absent from the national consciousness. The precise character of that destiny, however, as well as the ultimate goal to which it points, has varied with changing ideas and circumstances. One of its earliest forms was geographical determinism. Certain contiguous areas were thought of as surely destined for annexation because their location made them naturally part of the United States. . . .

What were the "natural boundaries" of the young republic? One mode of determining them was defined by Jefferson. Writing to Madison in 1809 of the hope of acquiring Cuba, he said: "Cuba can be defended by us without a navy, and this develops the principle which ought to limit our views. Nothing should ever be accepted which would require a navy to defend it." Northwardly, Jefferson visioned Canada as eventually to be drawn under the American flag; southwardly, Florida, Cuba, and probably Texas. On the west he apparently thought of the Rocky Mountains as forming the natural boundary. The West Coast would be peopled "with free and independent Americans, unconnected with us but by the ties of blood and interest and employing like us the rights of self-government.". . .

Such restricted ideas of the nation's natural boundaries were not to survive for many years. . . . It was inevitable that the coming of the railroad and, later, of the telegraph should result in an expanding conception of the nation's natural boundaries. Daniel Webster could still maintain in 1845 that there would arise an independent "Pacific republic" on the west coast, but for many others the "throne of Terminus" had moved on from the Rockies to the shores of the Pacific. The *Democratic Review*, leading organ of the expansionists of the Mexican War era, predicted in 1845 that a

railroad to the Pacific would soon be a reality, and that "the day cannot be far distant which shall witness the conveyance of the representatives from Oregon and California to Washington within less time than a few years ago was devoted to a similar journey by those from Ohio." The telegraph, furthermore, would soon enable Pacific coast newspapers "to set up in type the first half of the President's Inaugural, before the echoes of the latter half shall have died away beneath the lofty porch of the Capitol, as spoken from his lips." In the debate on the Oregon question in the House of Representatives in January, 1846, the significance of the Pacific as a natural boundary was repeatedly stressed. From the Atlantic to the Pacific, said Bowlin of Missouri, "we were by nature, ay, we were stamped by the hand of God himself, as one nation of men." Similarly, in the debate of 1844 and 1845 over the annexation of Texas, the Rio Grande with the neighboring strips of desert country had been portrayed as the divinely fixed natural boundary of the United States on the southwest.

If a divine hand had shaped the outlines of the North American continent with a view to its attaining political unity, the divine mind was thought to be by no means indifferent to the type of political organism which should dominate it. The American god of the early nineteenth century was the God of Democracy, and his followers had no doubt that he had reserved the continent for a democratic nation. Jefferson may not have regarded this consummation as a divinely appointed destiny, but he certainly contemplated as probable and desirable the spread of democratic institutions throughout the continent. The true flowering of this idea, however, belongs properly to the Jacksonian era, and its most enthusiastic exponent was the *Democratic Review*, a monthly magazine founded and for many years edited by Mr. John L. O'Sullivan. This exuberant Irish-American, whose faith in the institutions of his adopted country was irrepressible, not only coined the phrase "manifest destiny" but for years expounded in the pages of the *Review* the idea which it embodied.

The *Democratic Review* was founded in 1837. In the issue for November, 1839, appeared an article, presumably by O'Sullivan, entitled "The Great Nation of Futurity." This role was to be America's, it was argued,

because the principle upon which a nation is organized fixes its destiny, and that of equality is perfect, is universal. . . . . Besides, the truthful annals of any nation furnish abundant evidence, that its happiness, its greatness, its duration, were always proportionate to the democratic equality in its system of government. . . . . We point to the everlasting truth on the first page of our national declaration, and we proclaim to the millions of other lands, that "the gates of hell"— the powers of aristocracy and monarchy—"shall not prevail against it."

Thus happily founded upon the perfect principle of equality, the United States was destined to a unique success. Her shining example should "smite unto death the tyranny of kings, hierarchs, and oligarchs." What all this portended for the future boundaries of the United States the writer did not state except in poetic language. "Its floor shall be a hemisphere," he wrote, "its roof the firmament of the star-studded heavens, and its congregation an Union of many Republics, comprising hundreds of happy millions,. . . .governed by God's natural and moral law of equality. . . . ." Within a few years, however, the *Democratic Review* became sufficiently concrete in its ideas of the extent of the democratizing mission of the United States. Texas, Oregon, California, Canada, and much or all of Mexico, were to receive the blessings of American principles. The American continent had been reserved by Providence for the dawn of a new era, when men should be ready to throw off the antique systems of Europe and live in the light of equality and reason. The time was now at hand, and no American should shrink from the task of spreading the principles of liberty over all the continent. Cuba, too, had been left by Providence in the hands of a weak power until the United States was ready for it. Now it, like the rest, was "about to be annexed to the model republic."

The ideas so fervently preached in the *Democratic Review* were echoed in Congress and elsewhere. With reference to the Oregon controversy, James Buchanan asserted in 1844 that Providence had given to the American people the mission of "extending the blessings of Christianity and of civil and religious liberty over the whole North American continent." Breese of Illinois declared that "the impartial and the just" would see in the occupation of Oregon "a desire only to extend more widely the area of human freedom, ... as an extension, sir, of that grand theatre, on which God, in his providence, and in his own appointed time, intends to work out that high destiny he has assigned for the whole human race." California was not forgotten. A letter from an American in that Mexican state, published in the *Baltimore Patriot*, commented on the way in which "our people, like a sure heavy and sullen tide, are overflowing the country"; and the writer declared that, while not himself an advocate of territorial aggression, he thought he could "foresee in the inevitable destiny of this territory, one of the most efficient fortresses from which new and liberal are to combat old and despotic institutions." Kaufman of Texas was sure the day was near "when not one atom of kingly power will disgrace the North American continent." Apologists for the war with

Mexico were apt at urging its providential character and beneficent results. B. F. Porter, of Alabama, in an article on "The Mission of America," intimated that the war was a divine instrument for spreading American institutions and ideals to the Pacific; and Robert J. Walker, Secretary of the Treasury, inserted in his report for December, 1847, a paragraph gratefully acknowledging the aid of a "higher than any earthly power" which had guided American expansion in the past and which "still guards and directs our destiny, impels us onward, and has selected our great and happy country as a model and ultimate centre of attraction for all the nations of the world."

Neither natural boundaries nor divinely favored institutions were in themselves sufficient to insure the peopling of the continent by the favored race. The third essential factor was seen in what more than one Congressman termed "the American multiplication table." "Go to the West," said Kennedy of Indiana in 1846, "and see a young man with his mate of eighteen; after the lapse of thirty years, visit him again and instead of two, you will find twenty-two. This is what I call the American multiplication table.". . .

It was partly, too, upon the basis of this unexampled growth in numbers that the editor of the Democratic Review founded his doctrine of "manifest destiny." It was in an unsigned article in the number for July-August, 1845, that the phrase first appeared. The writer charged foreign nations with attempting to impede the annexation of Texas, with the object of "checking the fulfilment of our manifest destiny to overspread the continent allotted by Providence for the free development of our yearly multiplying millions." Texas, he said, had been

absorbed into the Union in the inevitable fulfilment of the general law which is rolling our

population westward; the connexion of which with that ratio of growth in population which is destined within a hundred years to swell our numbers to the enormous population of *two hundred and fifty millions* (if not more), is too evident to leave us in doubt of the manifest design of Providence in regard to the occupation of this continent.

When war with Mexico came, and the more rabid expansionists were seeking excuses for annexing large portions of Mexican territory, a different side of the idea of racial superiority was advanced. The Mexicans, it seemed, had a destiny too—how different from that of their northern neighbors! "The Mexican race," said the *Democratic Review*, "now see, in the fate of the aborigines of the north, their own inevitable destiny. They must amalgamate and be lost in the superior vigor of the Anglo-Saxon race, or they must utterly perish." The *New York Evening Post* indorsed the idea, sanctifying it in the name of Providence. "Providence has so ordained it; and it is folly not to recognize the fact. The Mexicans are *aboriginal Indians*, and they must share the destiny of their race."

This pre-Darwinian version of the "survival of the fittest" was branded by the aged Albert Gallatin, an opponent of the war, as "a most extraordinary assertion." That it persisted, that it constituted, in the 1850's, an integral part of the concept of manifest destiny is clear from the remarks of both friends and foes. John L. O'Sullivan was serving in 1855 as United States minister to Portugal. He reported to Secretary Marcy a conversation with some French imperialists in which he had said:

I should be as glad to see our common race and blood overspread all Africa under the French flag and all India under the British, as they ought to be to see it overspread all the Western hemisphere under ours;—and that probably enough that was the plan of Providence; to which we in America were accustomed to give the name of "manifest destiny."

On the other hand, George Fitzhugh of Virginia, who believed in institutions (such as slavery) for the protection of weaker races, charged the members of the "Young American" party in Congress with boasting "that the Anglo-Saxon race is manifestly destined to eat out all the other races, as the wire-grass destroys and takes the place of other grasses," and with inviting admiration for "this war of nature"—admiration which Fitzhugh, for one, refused to concede.

Thus manifest destiny, which must be thought of as embracing all the ideas hitherto considered—geographical determinism, the superiority of democratic institutions, the superior fecundity, stamina, and ability of the white race—became a justification for almost any addition of territory which the United States had the will and the power to obtain.

Such ideas were not, as has been rather generally assumed, peculiarly southern. In their extreme form, at least, both the ideas and the imperialistic program which they were used to justify were repudiated by southern Whig leaders, and even by John C. Calhoun himself. The southerner most closely associated with the program, Robert J. Walker, was of northern birth, was by no means an unwavering supporter of slavery, and was presently to sever entirely his connections with the South. The inventor of the phrase "manifest destiny" and one of the most persevering advocates of expansion was, as has been said, John L. O'Sullivan, who described himself in a letter to Calhoun as a "New York Free Soiler"; and he had the friendship and sympathy of prominent northern Democrats like Buchanan, Marcy, and Pierce. Indeed, if the manifest destiny of the 1840's and 1850's must be classified, it should be de-

scribed as Democratic rather than sectional. Yet, even this generalization will not bear too close scrutiny, for William H. Seward, an antislavery Whig and Republican, was scarcely less intrigued by the idea than O'Sullivan himself. As early as 1846 he was predicting that the population of the United States was "destined to roll its resistless waves to the icy barriers of the North, and to encounter oriental civilization on the shores of the Pacific"; and in a speech at St. Paul, Minnesota, in 1860, he asserted with assurance that Russian, Canadian, and Latin on the American continents were but laying the foundations for future states of the American republic, whose ultimate capital would be the City of Mexico.

Seward, in fact, supplies the chief link between the manifest destiny of the pre-Civil War years and the expansionist schemes of the decade following the war. As Secretary of State he had an opportunity to try his hand at a program of expansion; and though of all his plans the purchase of Alaska alone was carried through, the discussions of that and of other proposed acquisitions—the Danish West Indies, the Dominican Republic, the Hawaiian Islands, and Canada—demonstrated the continuity of ideas from 1850 to 1870. Professor T. C. Smith, who made an analysis of the expansionist arguments used in this period, found annexations urged on four principal grounds: economic value, strategic value to the navy, extension of republican institutions, and geographic determinism. Only the second of these—the naval base argument—was at all new. It owed its vogue at the time to the navy's difficulties during the war. The first was always to be met with, and the third and fourth were carryovers from the days of manifest destiny.

The collapse of the expansionist program of Seward and Grant was followed by a general loss of interest in such enterprises, which did not recover their one-time popularity until the era of the Spanish-American War. In the meantime, however, new arguments were taking shape which would eventually impinge on the popular consciousness and raise almost as keen an interest in expansion as that which had elected Polk in 1844. But while manifest destiny was a product indigenous to the United States, some of the new doctrines owed their origin to European trends of thought.

In 1859 Charles Darwin published his *Origin of Species*, setting forth the hypothesis that the evolution of the higher forms of life had come about through the preservation and perpetuation of chance variations by the "survival of the fittest" in the never ending struggle for existence. The authoritativeness of this work, and the stir which it made in the scientific world, gave a scientific sanction to the idea that perpetual struggle in the political and social world would lead upward along the evolutionary path. Many were the applications that might be made of such a principle— especially by nations and peoples considering themselves highly "fit." A nation with a faith in its political, moral, or racial superiority might take pleasure in the thought that in crushing its inferior neighbors it was at once obeying the law of destiny and contributing to the perfection of the species.

What did Darwinism signify for the future of the United States? One of the first to attempt an answer to that riddle was the historian, John Fiske, who spoke with double authority as a student of American institutions and a follower and popularizer of Darwin. Fiske's conclusion was sufficiently gratifying. Anglo-Saxons in the United States had evolved the "fittest" of all political principles—federalism—upon which all the world would at some future day be organized. Anglo-Saxons, moreover, excelled not only in institutions but in

growth of numbers and economic power. So evident was the superior "fitness" of this race that its expansion was certain to go on "until every land on the earth's surface that is not already the seat of an old civilization shall become English in its language, in its religion, in its political habits and traditions, and to a predominant extent in the blood of its people." "The day is at hand," said Fiske, "when four-fifths of the human race will trace its pedigree to English forefathers, as four-fifths of the white people of the United States trace their pedigree today." This was surely encouraging doctrine to Americans or British who wanted an excuse to go a-conquering.

Conclusions very similar to Fiske's were reached by Josiah Strong, a Congregational clergyman, who in 1885 published what became a popular and widely read book entitled *Our Country: Its Possible Future and Its Present Crisis*. The Anglo-Saxon, thought Strong, as the chief representative of the two most valuable civilizing forces— civil liberty and "a pure *spiritual* Christianity"—was being divinely schooled for "*the final competition of races. . . . .*" "If I read not amiss," he said, "this powerful race will move down upon Mexico, down upon Central and South America, out upon the islands of the sea, over upon Africa and beyond. And can any one doubt that the result of this competition of races will be the 'survival of the fittest'?" The extinction of inferior races before the conquering Anglo-Saxon might appear sad to some; but Strong knew of nothing likely to prevent it, and he accepted it as part of the divine plan. His doctrine was a curious blending of religious and scientific dogma.

If Fiske and Strong could show that expansion was a matter of destiny, another scholar of the day preached it as a duty. In his *Political Science and Comparative Constitutional Law*, published in 1890, John W. Burgess, of Columbia University, surveyed the political careers of the principal civilized races and concluded that, of them all, only the Teutonic group had talent of the highest order. Greek and Roman, Slav and Celt, had exhibited their various abilities. Some had excelled in building city-states; others, in planning world-empires. Only Teutons had learned the secret of the national state, the form fittest to survive. The Teutonic nations— German and Anglo-Saxon—were "the political nations *par excellence*," and this pre-eminence gave them the right "in the economy of the world to assume the leadership in the establishment and administration of states." Especially were they called "to carry the political civilization of the modern world into those parts of the world inhabited by unpolitical and barbaric races; i.e. they must have a colonial policy." There was "no human right to the status of barbarism." If barbaric peoples resisted the civilizing efforts of the political nations, the latter might rightly reduce them to subjection or clear their territory of their presence. If a population were not barbaric but merely incompetent politically, then too the Teutonic nations might "righteously assume sovereignty over, and undertake to create state order for, such a politically incompetent population."

There is in these pages of Burgess such a complete justification not only for British and German imperialism but also for the course of acquiring colonies and protectorates upon which the United States was to embark in 1898 that one learns with surprise from his rather naïve autobiography that Burgess was profoundly shocked by the war with Spain and felt that the adoption of an imperialistic career was a colossal blunder. One would have supposed that he would have rejoiced that his country was assuming its share of world-responsibility as one of the Teutonic nations.

To Fiske and Strong, expansion was destiny; to Burgess, it was duty, though he apparently excused his own country from any share in its performance. To Alfred Thayer Mahan, the historian and prophet who frankly assumed the role of propagandist, it was both duty and opportunity. Mahan's *Influence of Sea Power upon History*, the result of a series of lectures at the Naval War College at Newport, Rhode Island, was published in 1890. Other books on naval history followed, but it is likely that Mahan reached a wider American public through the many magazine articles which he published at frequent intervals during the ensuing decade. History, as Mahan wrote it, was no mere academic exercise. Searching the past for lessons applicable to the here and now, he found them in full measure. Rather, he found *one*, which he never tired of driving home: Sea power was essential to national greatness. Sea power embraced commerce, merchant marine, navy, naval bases whence commerce might be protected, and colonies where it might find its farther terminals. One nation, Great Britain, had learned this lesson by heart and practiced it faithfully, with results that Mahan thought admirable. One other nation, he hoped, might walk in her footsteps.

Certain specific needs, beside the obvious one of a stronger navy and better coast defenses, Mahan urged upon his countrymen. If an Isthmian canal were to be built, the United States ought to build and control it, or, failing this, to control completely the approaches to it. This involved a willingness to accept islands in the Caribbean whenever they could be had by righteous means; sheer acts of conquest Mahan repudiated. It involved also a willingness to accept the Hawaiian Islands, partly as an outpost to the Pacific end of the canal, partly for another reason which weighed heavily with Mahan. The Pacific, he believed, was to be the theater of a vast conflict between Occident and Orient, with the United States holding the van of the Western forces. His deep religious sense assured him that the Deity was preparing the Christian powers for that coming cataclysm, but he was equally sure that mere human agents must keep their powder dry. The United States must be ready, with a navy, a canal, and as many island outposts as she could righteously acquire, for her share in the great struggle between civilizations and religions. Even the practical-minded naval officer must have a cosmic justification for the policy of national imperialism which he advocated.

It was such ideas as these of Fiske, Strong, Burgess, and Mahan which created a public opinion receptive to expansion overseas in 1898. Theodore Roosevelt and Henry Cabot Lodge, whose influence upon the events of that year was large indeed, were under the spell of Mahan's writings. Roosevelt had been a pupil of Burgess while studying law at Columbia. In the debate over imperialism which ensued, the argument from Anglo-Saxon or Teutonic superiority and the divinely appointed mission of the race was probably as influential as the more practical strategic and economic arguments. Kipling's contribution, "The White Man's Burden," which appeared in 1898, fitted in well with the American temper. In the United States Senate, young Albert J. Beveridge, using language that might almost have been taken bodily from Burgess' treatise, declared that God "has made us [Anglo-Saxons and Teutons] the master organizers of the world to establish system where chaos reigns. . . . . He has made us adept in government that we may administer government among savage and senile peoples." William Allen White, in the *Emporia Gazette*, proclaimed: "Only Anglo-Saxons can govern themselves. . . . . It is the Anglo-Saxon's manifest destiny to go

forth as a world conqueror. He will take possession of the islands of the sea. . . . . This is what fate holds for the chosen people." Senator O. H. Platt wrote President McKinley that in Connecticut "those who believe in Providence, see, or think they see, that God has placed upon this Government the solumn duty of providing for the people of these islands [the Philippines] a government based upon the principle of liberty no matter how many difficulties the problem may present." A missionary from China was quoted as saying: "You will find that all American missionaries are in favor of expansion."

Even those who stressed the economic value of new possessions could not refrain from claiming the special interest of Providence. That the war with Spain and the victory in the Philippines should have come just as the European powers were attempting to partition China and monopolize its markets, seemed to the *American Banker* of New York "a coincidence which has a providential air." Familiar to all students of the period is McKinley's story of how he prayed for divine guidance as to the disposition of the Philippines, and of how "one night it came to me this way—I don't know how it was but it came: . . . .that we could not turn them over to France or Germany—our commercial rivals in the Orient—that would be bad business and discreditable." Reasons of a more ideal character were vouchsafed to William McKinley on the same occasion, but McKinley's God did not hesitate to converse with him in terms that might better have befitted Mark Hanna. Perhaps McKinley did not misunderstand. Josiah Strong was a clergyman and hence in a better position that McKinley to interpret the wishes of the Deity; yet he found in Providence a concern for American business similar to that which McKinley detected. Strong, too, had in mind the Philippines and especially their relation to China and to the maintenance of the Open Door in the markets of that developing empire.

And when we remember [he wrote] that our new necessities [markets for our manufactures] are precisely complementary to China's new needs, it is not difficult to see a providential meaning in the fact that, with no design of our own, we have become an Asiatic power, close to the Yellow Sea, and we find it easy to believe that

"There's a divinity that shapes our ends,
Rough-hew them how we will."

Expansionists of different periods had invoked a God of Nature, a God of Democracy, a God of Evolution. It seems appropriate enough that those who inaugurated the last phase of territorial expansion, at the close of the nineteenth century, should have proclaimed their faith in a God of Business.

A diplomatic historian at the University of Wisconsin (Milwaukee), CHARLES VEVIER (1924-   ) points out that throughout the nineteenth century Americans argued that expansion of the nation's commercial opportunities abroad was necessary if its domestic economic potential was to develop. And in the 1890s, Alfred Thayer Mahan and Brooks Adams turned to these historical arguments in their efforts to promote overseas expansion. By focusing on the history of ideas instead of events, Vevier tends to minimize the degree to which the expansionism of the 1890s marked a sharp break with the American past. But can American expansion be understood by separating ideas from events? And were the events of 1898 and 1899 intricately tied to the expansionist tradition of previous decades?*

American Continentalism

Ideology is the means by which a nation bridges the gap between its domestic achievement and its international aspiration. American continentalism, as the term is used here, provided just such an order of ideology and national values. It consisted of two related ideas. First, it regarded the United States as possessing identical "national and imperial boundaries.". . . Second, it viewed much of North America as a stage displaying the evolving drama of a unique political society, distinct from that of Europe and glowing in the white light of manifest destiny. This attitude sharpened the practice of American foreign policy. Encountering the opposition of Europe's powers, it asserted that the United States was engaged in a do-

mestic and therefore inevitable policy of territorial extension across the continent. . . . Relying on its separation from the Old World, the United States redefined the conventional terms of foreign relations by domesticating its foreign policy.

But sharp and immediate disengagements in history are rare. Professor Norman Graebner has argued persuasively that the acquisition of Oregon and California—conventionally set within the background of territorial expansion to the west and guaranteed by manifest destiny—was due predominantly to maritime influence and executed by a President whose party represented the agrarian expansionism of Jefferson. In spite of its apparent territorial insularity, American continentalism was

*Reprinted from Charles Vevier, "American Continentalism: An Idea of Expansion, 1845-1910," *American Historical Review*, LXV (January, 1960), 323-335. Footnotes omitted.

bound to an older doctrine that had been overshadowed by the record of land acquisition of the 1840's. In these years, and in the 1850's as well, there were some men who were affected by the outlook of American continentalism and who adapted for their own ends the great objective of European expansion that dated from the age of Columbus and the Elizabethans. They sought to deepen commercial contact with Asia, an ambition that added a maritime dimension to the era of territorial expansion preceding the Civil War.

Students of American Far Eastern policy have already pointed out the rough coincidence of the westward movement across the continent with the rising activity of American interest in the Pacific Ocean and trade in China. By the early 1840's, Hawaii had already shifted into the continental orbit. Exploration of the Pacific Ocean had been undertaken by the government beginning with the Wilkes expedition in 1838 and concluding with the Ringgold voyages to the northern Pacific in 1853-1859. The Cushing Treaty with China in 1844 and the opening of Japan by Perry a decade later reflected the attraction of Far Eastern trade markets to American merchants on the Atlantic seaboard. The gold strike of 1849 stimulated railroad passage across the Isthmus of Panama, encouraged shipping operations between New York and California, and suggested continuation of this traffic to the Orient. The wider commercial possibilities implied by these forces meshed with an older American interest in the Caribbean, particularly in Cuba and the picket line of West Indian islands that ran down to Latin America. In an age of the clipper ship and the steady reduction of the tariff at the behest of agrarian elements, these developments drew taut the strand of national mercantile expansionist ambition that seemingly had lain slack while the territorial lines of American continentalism

were cast westward across North America. This added tension suggested to some that the United States was linked to the historic expansionism of Europe westward to Asia, that it was the fulfillment of the long search for a "passage to India," and that a great mercantile empire could be developed on the basis of Asian commerce.

Historians have been prone to examine American expansionism in terms of conflicting mercantile and agrarian interests. They have overlooked the presence of a unifying view of American world geographical centralism that was grounded in a "geopolitical" interpretation of American continentalism and its place in the history of Europe's expansion to Asia. What emerged was a combination of two deterministic patterns of thought reflected in the outlook of such men as William Gilpin, Asa Whitney, Matthew Fontaine Maury, and Perry McDonough Collins. These men shaped an expectation of commercial empire as an end in itself as well as a means of developing the internal continental empire. Today, after the bitter experiences of its practice in the 1930's, geopolitics deservedly has an unsavory reputation. Although it did not exist in any organized form or established theory before the Civil War, it was, nevertheless, a conceptual instrument whose economic implications projected American continentalism onto the world scene and anticipated in some respects its greater use by the expansionists of 1898.

William Gilpin, "America's first Geopolitician," declared that the unifying geographical features of the North American continent, particulary the Mississippi Valley, contrasted favorably with Europe and Asia. A summary of his views in the period 1846-1849 reveals his belief that the physical environment of America promised the growth of an area equal in population and resources to that of the entire world. A

Jeffersonian democrat and a devotee of the writings of Alexander von Humboldt, he believed in the inevitable westward march of an agrarian civilization to the Pacific Ocean. He also associated westward expansion with American commerce and whaling enterprise already established there. During the Oregon crisis in 1846, Gilpin advised congressmen, as he may have suggested to President James Polk, that settlers moving into Oregon from the Mississippi Valley, the geographically favored heart of the continent, would make the mouth of the Columbia River an outlet for the export of American farm produce to Asia. Since agriculture sought through commerce an "infinite market of consumption" in the Far East, Oregon became the "maritime wing of the Mississippi Valley upon the Pacific, as New England was on the Atlantic." A strong bid for Asian trade, therefore, depended on the construction of a transcontinental railroad from the Mississippi to the Columbia River that would link the agricultural heart of the North American continent with the Pacific Ocean. By developing the interior, thereby gaining access to the coast, the United States might become the center of a new world traffic pattern. . . .

The Pacific railroad, in fact, was closely identified with the career of Asa Whitney, who had returned from China after a successful career as a merchant and who had campaigned from 1845 onward for the construction of a railroad from the upper portion of the Mississippi Valley to Oregon. It was Whitney's project that dominated for five years the great American debate over this vital internal transportation scheme. Unless Oregon was bound to the rest of the country by a transcontinental railroad, Whitney warned, the nation would be forced to engage in a balance-of-power diplomacy in the European manner, an eventuality that he thought would destroy the

continental homogeneity of America. In presenting his Pacific railway scheme, he proposed to connect Oregon with the rest of the country, open oriental trade marts to American commerce and agriculture, particularly if the railroad was tied to a Pacific Ocean shipping line, and provide an instrument for the internal development of the nation-continent that would serve as "the means, and only means, by which the vast wilderness between civilization and Oregon can be settled." Thus he exalted the continental potential of producing "the most necessary and important products of the earth—bread stuffs and meat," and stressed the value of an international "commerce of reciprocity—an exchange of commodities." The railroad, he insisted, would "revolutionize the entire commerce of the world; placing us directly in the centre of all. . . , all must be tributary to us, and, in a moral point of view, it will be the means of civilizing and Christianizing all mankind."

Matthew Fontaine Maury, hydrographer of the United States Navy and adviser on railroad and international commercial problems to southern businessmen and politicians, was also interested in the relationship of the Pacific railroad issue to the old dream of the "passage to India." But he formulated a wider geopolitical conception of the North American continent by linking it with Latin America as well as with Asia. He agreed that a Pacific railroad was needed to develop the continental interior as a means of raising land values, encouraging settlement of the western lands, and providing for the continental defense of the nation. He, too, shared the conviction of the importance of the Asian trade and, faithful to the interests of the South, he pressed for the construction of a transcontinental railroad from Memphis to Monterey.

Maury, however, was influenced by an old geographical-historical idea that river valley civilizations were the most enduring and fruitful forms of society. In his view, the basins of the Mississippi and the Amazon Rivers were united in a vast continental-maritime complex that depended upon American supremacy of the Gulf of Mexico and the Caribbean Sea, the "American Mediterranean" as he called it. Aware of the potential of an age of steam, he believed that conventional ideas of geographical relationships had to change. Maury urged Americans to think of ocean navigation around the globe in terms of great circle travel rather than of routes laid out on the Mercator projection. This placed his Memphis-Monterey transcontinental railroad project that was to service the Mississippi Valley close to the great circle running from Central America to Shanghai at a point off the coast of California. Cut a canal through the Isthmus of Panama that would link the Pacific Ocean with the "American Mediterranean" and the shortened route to Asia would force European commerce to use a passageway that Maury insisted should never be under the control of a foreign power since it violated traditional American policy to allow foreign interference in the Western Hemisphere. "I regard the Pacific railroad and a commercial thoroughfare across the Isthmus as links in the same chain, parts of the great whole which. . .is to effect a revolution in the course of trade. . . .Those two works. . .are not only necessary fully to develop the immense resources of the Mississippi valley. . .but. . .their completion would place the United States on the summit level of commerce. . . ." In effect, Maury extended the line of American continental interest south from the Mississippi in order to command the same degree of geographic centralism that had marked the ideas of Gilpin and Whitney. The canal, taken in conjunction with the Pacific railroad, demonstrated his ambition for the

United States to overcome the "barrier that separates us from the markets of six hundred millions of people—three-fourths of the population of the earth. Break it down. . .and this country is placed midway between Europe and Asia; this sea [Gulf of Mexico and the Caribbean] becomes the centre of the world and the focus of the world's commerce."

This doctrine of geopolitical centralism was reflected in the activity of Perry McDonough Collins, whose career had been shaped by the westward movement, experience with steamship operations on the Mississippi, and the California gold rush. Living on the West Coast in the 1850's, he not only absorbed the impact of the nation's new geographical position on the Pacific but also read about Russia's explorations of the northern Pacific Ocean and its expansion into eastern Siberia. Quickly he "fixed upon the river Amoor in Eastern Siberia as the destined channel by which American commercial enterprise was to penetrate the obscure depths of Northern Asia.". . .

Collins inspired Western Union's project for the construction of an international overland telegraph system through British Columbia, Alaska, and Siberia in 1865 which was to be linked with Russia's own network to Europe. Basic to the whole scheme was the anticipation that the transcontinental telegraph line to the Pacific built by Western Union in 1860-1861 would be in the center of the vast enterprise. "Consequently," ran one of the company's circulars, "when the extension line of this company shall be completed the commerce of the whole of Europe, Asia, and North America, radiating from their great commercial centers will be tributary to it."

The outlook formulated by these various opinions suggests the existence of two related American worlds. The first was the

nation-continent created through the interaction of foreign policy and territorial
expansion that resulted in the acquisition of
contiguous territory in North America. In
turn, it projected the concept of the second
American world, the continental domain
that was fated to extend its influence over
the entire world through the expansion of
commerce and control of international
communications. The relations of both
worlds were reciprocal. All this, however,
depended upon realizing the economic
implications of the central position con-
ferred upon the United States through its
expansion in North America and the significance of this event in the general expansionist history of the European world.

By the middle of the 1850's, aspects of
this informal system of geopolitical thought
had made its impression upon public discussion, affecting debates over internal
communication and transportation as well
as foreign policy. It is true, however, that
the notion of an American "empire" based
on the idea of the United States as the great
land bridge to Asia had given way to the
growing tension of the sectional debates
over federal policy dealing with the development of the continental interior. Nevertheless, the fund of ideas that had projected
American continentalism onto the world
scene were restated and maintained by
William Henry Seward, an expansionist, a
worshipper of the continental tradition established and exemplified earlier by John
Quincy Adams, and a man whose outlook
matched the geopolitical determinism exhibited by Gilpin, Whitney, Maury, and
Collins.

Ten years before Seward became Secretary of State, he advocated the construction of a Pacific railroad and telegraph
in the debates over the admission of California to the Union. Americans who understood the benign future of the American
continent, Seward argued, had to prevent a

division between the North and the South
in order to overcome the more portentous
split between East and West caused by the
expansion of the United States. Centralized
political unity, the economic welfare of the
continental empire, and mastery of the seas
that bounded the great land mass between
two worlds—these were required if the
United States was to take effective advantage of its geographical position to
direct commerce with Europe and "in-
tercept" trade with the Far East. . . .

This rhetoric was not separated from the
realities that Seward encountered as Secretary of State. The continent under American dominion, he reported, "like every
other structure of large proportions," required "outward buttresses" that were strategically favorable to the United States.
Thus the policy of attempting to buy naval
installations in the Caribbean after the
Civil War reflected his conviction at the
outbreak of the conflict that Spanish intrusion in the region partially justified the
launching of a propaganda counterattack
throughout Latin America as well as war
against Spain. In 1864, he insisted that
commerce and communication in North
America were centralized in the United
States and had to be extended as a means of
uniting domestic and foreign commerce
and encouraging the development of American "agricultural, forest, mineral, and
marine resources." It was Seward who
wrote the vital provisions of the
Burlingame Treaty of 1868 with China that
provided for the importation of Chinese
coolies to work on the transcontinental
railroad and western mining undertakings.
He also contributed to the continental basis
of the argument used by Senator Charles
Sumner, who supported the purchase of
Alsaska by pointing out that the new territory rounded off the continental domain
and permitted contact with Far Eastern
markets by the shortest possible sea route

from the West Coast. Later Seward made his meaning more clear to Canadians when he implied that the Alaskan purchase was a portent of "commerical and political forces" that made "permanent political separation of British Columbia from Alaska and the Washington territory impossible." And, it was Seward's system of roughhewn continental geopolitics and beliefs cut out of the American grain that gives depth to the vigor with which he pursued American interests in the Far East. Much of his ambitious program, however, was not fulfilled because, as he said, "no new national policy deliberately undertaken upon considerations of future advantages ever finds universal favor when first announced.". . .

Mahan might well have added, however, that it was his geopolitics as well as that of Brooks Adams that defined the "field of collision." For the serious domestic crisis in the United States occurring in the 1890's within the context of a global economy and an international transportation revolution forecast a pessimitic future. Each, in his own way, attempted to swamp it with a conception of the past that he carried with him. Both Mahan's quest for a new mercantilism and Adams' propaganda for a new empire illustrate a retreat into history for a model that might avert disaster. One theme emerged—the extension of the nation's economic power from the line of the West Indies, Panama, and Hawaii to Asia. Here, the expansionist projection of the American continental experience that was developed in the pre-Civil War period acquired some relevance in the outlook of Brooks Adams. Viewing the expansion of Europe and of the United States as complementary developments, he turned to geopolitics to explain the nature of the problem.

The Germans and the Russians appeared ready to march to the East. This move would reverse the historical westward trend of the exchanges that formed the basis of world power. Obsessed by the belief that control over Asia and its resources was the issue between the Russo-German bloc and what he believed to be a weakened England, Adams called for an Anglo-American rapproachement. This would allow the geographical center of the exchanges to "cross the Atlantic and aggrandize America." The result? "Probably," Adams suggested, "human society would then be absolutely dominated by a vast combination of peoples whose right wing would rest upon the British Isles, whose left would overhang the middle province of China, whose centre would approach the Pacific, and who encompass the Indian Ocean as though it were a lake, much as the Romans encompassed the Mediterranean." Specifically, Adams, Mahan, and the imperial expansionists who clustered around Theodore Roosevelt urged upon the United States the "large policy of 1898," which revived the Caribbean-Panama-Pacific Ocean relationship that had been sketched out in the 1840's and 1850's and publicized by Seward. But by 1909, the outer edges of this grandiose empire were frayed by abrasive realities in Asia. The failure of the open door in China, the knowledge that the Phillippines could not be defended, the growing tension with Japan over Manchuria—all this was complicated by the existence of the ideological *Realpolitik* of Theodore Roosevelt, who claimed American manipulative power over affairs in Asia but who was cautious enough to realize that he did not have it. Roosevelt's refusal to carry out completely Adams' program drove Adams back to examine his own nationalist assumptions in a biography of his grandfather that he never completed.

At this point in his quest, the traditional elements of American continentalism received a full statement—geographical determinism, political and social separation from Europe, and independent action in foreign affairs. Nevertheless, Adams, like Mahan, continued to interpret the history of American continentalism as an expression of eighteenth-century mercantilist imperialism. Just as Asia appeared in his own time to be the principal objective that would guarantee survival through expansion, so North America had appeared to the European powers. "Men believed that he who won America might aspire to that universal empire which had been an ideal since the dawn of civilization." Franklin, Washington, and John Quincy Adams had understood the need for a consolidated, unified, and expansionist state strong enough to establish itself in North America. In 1823, the Monroe Doctrine confirmed what the American Revolution had already demonstrated: the leadership of the westward march of the exchanges would pass from a divided Europe to a unified America. "It was the first impressive manifestation of that momentous social movement which has recently culminated in the migration of the centre of the equilibrium of human society across the Atlantic." Here the nationalist met the imperialist when the expansionist projection of continentalism made clear that America, the prize of empire in the eighteenth century, had to become an empire in the twentieth century.

Contemporary students of the United States foreign policy that developed at the turn of the century are confronted with a problem of perspective. From the standpoint of the expansionist projection of American continentalism revealed in the pre-Civil War era, the imperialism of McKinley and Roosevelt was not a new departure in American history. It was not an "aberration" of national behavior which has been loosely defined as the emergence of the United States to world power. The geopolitical suggestions of Mahan and Brooks Adams helped American statesmen to install the United States as such a power. It was also a startling demonstration of the adjustment of the new ideological justifications of the 1890's to an older nationalistic expansionist base formulated by men of an earlier generation. Gilpin, Whitney, Maury, and Collins had sensed the meaning of the new technology, its effect upon geographical relationships, and the interrelations between aspects of the economic system at home, and these men were captured by a desire to assume the leadership of an entire Western civilization in order to make a lasting impression upon Asia.

Historians who are sensitive to the relationship of foreign and domestic affairs as well as to the play of ideas upon foreign policy might do well to reexamine and explore the concept of American continentalism as an ideology of overseas expansion. Conventionally employed to explain the separatist and isolationist quality of the American outlook on world affairs in the nineteenth century, American continentalism also possessed a geopolitical character—natively derived in large measure—that was contrary to its own spirit. The only virtue of geopolitics is that it draws attention to the facts of political geography; its greatest vice is that it lends itself to almost mystical judgments of national purpose in international affairs. Seemingly dealing with reality, it becomes a refuge for unclear and unfulfilled aspirations. Geographers long ago learned this bitter lesson. Historians of American foreign policy might profit by investigating further the active presence in nineteenth-century America of this aspect of thought, not as a justification for foreign policy but as an important stimulus of nationalist expansionism.

Twice winner of the Pulitzer Prize in history, RICHARD HOFSTADTER (1916-   ) of Columbia University has written widely on what he has called the "paranoid style of American politics." Focusing on the irrational basis underlying political action, his studies frequently reveal a distrust of popular democracy and egalitarian sentiments. Finding it difficult to view late-nineteenth-century expansionism as rationally calculated to achieve desirable goals, Hofstadter, in this essay, explains the jingoism of the 1890s as a frustrated response of various groups to the economic depression that started in 1893. But why did the Venezuelan boundary dispute provide an opportunity for various groups to vent their frustration? And why did the Cleveland Administration respond to national hysteria by taking the country to the brink of war?°

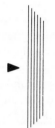

Depression and Psychic Crisis

The taking of the Philippine Islands from Spain in 1899 marked a major historical departure for the American people. It was a breach in their traditions and a shock to their established values. To be sure, from their national beginnings they had constantly engaged in expansion, but almost entirely into contiguous territory. Now they were extending themselves to distant extrahemispheric colonies; they were abandoning a strategy of defense hitherto limited to the continent and its appurtenances, in favor of a major strategic commitment in the Far East; and they were now supplementing the spread of a relatively homogeneous population into territories destined from the beginning for self-government with a far different procedure in which control was imposed by force on millions of ethnic aliens. The acquisition of the islands, therefore, was understood by contemporaries on both sides of the debate, as it is readily understood today, to be a turning-point in our history.

To discuss the debate in isolation from other events, however, would be to deprive it of its full significance. American entrance into the Philippine Islands was a by-product of the Spanish-American War. The Philippine crisis is inseparable from the war crisis, and the war crisis itself is inseparable from a larger constellation that might be called "the psychic crisis of the 1890's".

Central in the background of the psychic

°From Richard Hofstadter, "Manifest Destiny and the Philippines," reprinted by permission of the publisher from *America in Crisis*, edited by Daniel Aaron. Copyright 1952 by Alfred A. Knopf, Inc. Pp. 173-178. Footnotes omitted.

crisis was the great depression that broke in 1893 and was still very acute when the agitation over the war in Cuba began. Severe depression, by itself, does not always generate an emotional crisis as intense as that of the nineties. In the 1870's the country had been swept by a depression of comparable acuteness and duration which, however, did not give rise to all the phenomena that appeared in the 1890's or to very many of them with comparable intensity and impact. It is often said that the 1890's, unlike the 1870's, form some kind of a "watershed" in American history. The difference between the emotional and intellectual impact of these two depressions can be measured, I believe, not by any difference in severity, but rather by a reference to a number of singular events that in the 1890's converged with the depression to heighten its impact upon the public mind.

First in importance was the Populist movement, the free-silver agitation, the heated campaign of 1896. For the first time in our history a depression had created an allegedly "radical" movement strong enough to capture a major party and raise the specter, however unreal, of drastic social convulsion. Second was the maturation and bureaucratization of American business, the completion of its essential industrial plant, and the development of trusts on a scale sufficient to stir the anxiety that the old order of competitive opportunities was approaching an eclipse. Third, and of immense symbolic importance, was the apparent filling up of the continent and disappearance of the frontier line. We now know how much land had not yet been taken up and how great were the remaining possibilities of internal expansion both in business and on the land; but to the mind of the 1890's it seemed that the resource that had engaged the energies of the people for three centuries had been used up; the

frightening possibility suggested itself that a serious juncture in the nation's history had come. As Frederick Jackson Turner expressed it in his famous paper of 1893: "Now, four centuries from the discovery of America, at the end of one hundred years of life under the Constitution, the frontier has gone, and with its going has closed the first period of American history."

To middle-class citizens who had been brought up to think in terms of the nineteenth-century order, things looked bad. Farmers in the staple-growing region seemed to have gone mad over silver and Bryan; workers were stirring in bloody struggles like the Homestead and Pullman strikes; the supply of new land seemed at an end; the trust threatened the spirit of business enterprise; civic corruption was at a high point in the large cities; great waves of seemingly unassimilable immigrants arrived yearly and settled in hideous slums. To many historically conscious writers, the nation seemed overripe, like an empire ready for collapse through a stroke from outside or through internal upheaval. Acute as the situation was for all those who lived by the symbols of national power—for the governing and thinking classes—it was especially poignant for young people, who would have to make their careers in the dark world that seemed to be emerging.

The symptomatology of the crisis might record several tendencies in popular thought and behavior that had not been observable before or had existed only in pale and tenuous form. These symptoms fall into two basic moods. The key to one of them is an intensification of protest and humanitarian reform. Populism, Utopianism, the rise of the Christian Social gospel, the growing intellectual interest in Socialism, the social settlement movement that appealed so strongly to the college generation of the nineties, the quickening of protest in the realistic novel—all these are expressions of this mood. The other is one of national self-assertion, aggression, expansion. The tone of the first was sympathy, of the second, power. During the 1890's far more patriotic groups were founded than in any other decade of our history; the naval theories of Captain Mahan were gaining in influence; naval construction was booming; there was an immense quickening of the American cult of Napoleon and a vogue of the virile and martial writings of Rudyard Kipling; young Theodore Roosevelt became the exemplar of the vigorous, masterful, out-of-doors man; the revival of European imperialism stirred speculation over what America's place would be in the world of renewed colonial rivalries. But most significant was the rising tide of jingoism, a matter of constant comment among observers of American life during the decade.

Jingoism, of course, was not new in American history. But during the 1870's and '80's the American public had been notably quiescent about foreign relations. There had been expansionist statesmen, but they had been blocked by popular apathy and statecraft had been restrained. Grant had failed dismally in his attempt to acquire Santo Domingo; our policy toward troubled Hawaii had been cautious; in 1877 an offer of two Haitian naval harbors had been spurned. In responding to Haiti, Secretary of State Frelinghuysen had remarked that "the policy of this Government . . . has tended toward avoidance of possessions disconnected from the main continent." Henry Cabot Lodge, in his life of George Washington published in 1889, observed that foreign relations then filled "but a slight place in American politics, and excite generally only a languid interest." Within a few years this comment would have seemed absurd; the history of the

1890's is the history of public agitation over expansionist issues and of quarrels with other nations.

Three primary incidents fired American jingoism between the spring of 1891 and the close of 1895. First came Secretary of State Blaine's tart and provocative reply to the Italian minister's protest over the lynching of eleven Italians in New Orleans. Then there was friction with Chile over a riot in Valparaiso in which two American sailors were killed and several injured by a Chilean mob. In 1895 occurred the more famous Venezuela boundary dispute with Britain. Discussion of these incidents would take us too far afield, but note that they all had these characteristics in common: in none of them was national security or the national interest vitally involved; in all three American diplomacy was extraordinarily and disproportionately aggressive; in all three the possibility of war was contemplated; and in each case the American public and press response was enthusiastically nationalist.

It is hard to read the history of these events without concluding that politicians were persistently using jingoism to restore their prestige, mend their party fences, and divert the public mind from grave internal discontents. It hardly seems an accident that jingoism and Populism rose together. Documentary evidence for the political exploitation of foreign crises is not overwhelmingly abundant, in part because such a motive is not necessarily conscious and where it is conscious it is not likely to be confessed or recorded. The persistence of jingoism in every administration from Harrison's to Theodore Roosevelt's, however, is too suggestive to be ignored. During the nineties the press of each party was fond of accusing the other of exploiting foreign conflict. We know that Blaine was not

above twisting the British lion's tail for political purposes; and there is no reason to believe that he would have exempted Italy
from the same treatment. We know too that
Harrison, on the eve of the Chile affair, for
the acuteness of which he was primarily responsible, was being urged by prominent
Republican politicians who had the coming
Presidential campaign in mind to pursue a
more aggressive foreign policy because it
would "have the . . . effect of diverting attention from stagnant political discussions." And although some Democratic
papers charged that he was planning to run
for re-election during hostilities so that he
could use the "don't-swap-horses-in-the-
middle-of-the-stream" appeal, many Democrats felt that it was politically necessary
for them to back him against Chile so that,
as one of their Congressmen remarked, the
Republicans could not "run away with all
the capital there is to be made in an attempt
to assert national self-respect." Grover
Cleveland admittedly was a man of exceptional integrity whose stand against
pressure for the annexation of Hawaii
during 1893-4 does him much credit. But
precisely for this act of abnegation his administration fell under the charge made by
Republican jingoes like Lodge and by

many in his own party that he was indifferent to America's position in the world.
And if Cleveland was too high-minded a
man to exploit a needless foreign crisis, his
Secretary of State, Richard Olney, was not.
The Venezuela affair, which came at a very
low point in the prestige of Cleveland's
administration, offered Olney a rich chance
to prove to critics in both parties that the
administration was, after all, capable of vigorous diplomacy. That the crisis might
have partisan value was not unthinkable to
members of Olney's party. He received a
suggestive letter from a Texas Congressman encouraging him to "go ahead,"
on the ground that the Venezuela issue was
a "winner" in every section of the country.
"When you come to diagnose the country's
internal ills," his correspondent continued,
"the possibilities of 'blood and iron' loom
up immediately. Why, Mr. Secretary, just
think of how angry the anarchistic, socialistic, and populistic boil appears on our political surface and who knows how deep its
roots extend or ramify? One cannon shot
across the bow of a British boat in defense of
this principle will knock more *pus* out of it
than would suffice to innoculate and
corrupt our people for the next two centuries.". . .

Critics frequently charge that American foreign policy has
been shaped too much by the desire of policy makers to
please domestic pressure groups, that insufficient attention
has been given to the forces at work in the international
arena. In this essay, NELSON M. BLAKE (1908-   ), a
professor of history at Syracuse University, obliquely
makes a similar charge against the Cleveland
Administration in regard to the Venezuelan boundary
crisis. Even so, Blake does argue that Cleveland acted
partly from the belief that it was necessary for the United
States to defend the principles of the Monroe Doctrine. But
what did the Monroe Doctrine mean to Cleveland? Was he
willing to defend the principles of the Doctrine with war if
necessary? If so, why?*

Reaffirmation of
the Monroe Doctrine

Cleveland's Venezuelan policy, regarded
primarily as diplomacy, seems paradoxical.
Cleveland was one of the most conservative
of American presidents and not in the least
given to adventure in foreign affairs. Yet
the Olney note on the Venezuelan issue and
Cleveland's special message to Congress
are among the most crudely assertive ever
issued by responsible American statesmen.
How did it happen that caution so abruptly
became rashness? Even in the case of the
rugged Cleveland it must be remembered
that American foreign policy has always
been exposed to many forces extraneous to
diplomacy. Crosscurrents of political
pressure and mobilized opinion are usually
at work, and any particular step of American diplomacy may represent the re-

sultant of many forces. Here is the clue this
essay will follow in reviewing Cleveland's
Venezuelan policy.

In 1895 the tide of nineteenth century
imperialism was running strong. Under
Harrison and the energetic Blaine it had
seemed that the United States was about to
join the colonial race. Cleveland, however,
had set his face doggedly against this tendency. Particularly by repudiating the Republican policy in Hawaii the Democratic
President had demonstrated his repug-
nance for his predecessor's policy.

Cleveland's natural inclination toward
caution in foreign relations was supported
by the two men who held the most important American diplomatic appoint-
ments. Secretary of State Walter Q.

*Reprinted from Nelson M. Blake, "Background of Cleveland's Venezuelan Policy," *American Historical
Review*, XLVII (January, 1942), 259-277. Footnotes omitted.

Gresham was a friendly mid-Westerner who sought to conciliate and win over by argument the foreign representatives with whom he came in contact, while Thomas F. Bayard, our ambassador to Great Britain, had a kindred preference for the smooth path of gentlemanly compromise.

The predilection of Cleveland, Gresham, and Bayard for a quiet and unassertive foreign policy had a certain amount of support. Many of the mugwumps who had been attracted to Cleveland were typical nineteenth century liberals—free traders and anti-imperialists. Notable among these were Carl Schurz, Oscar Straus, and Edward Atkinson. The New York *Evening Post* and the *Nation*, both directed by E. L. Godkin, were sounding boards for this kind of opinion. Closely allied with this opposition to the diplomacy of force was a growing support for international arbitration.

Among those who had no great confidence in the proximity of the era of peace through free trade and arbitration there were a few who believed that the United States should become the ally of England. The Anglo-Saxons, they asserted, were favored by Providence with a special destiny and should stand together against the world. Such sentiments were not yet safe for politicians but were thrown out with some regularity by publicists. The assumption of Anglo-Saxon unity was to be met more frequently in England than in America. British isolation was already appearing dangerous, and American tourists and journalists in 1895 remarked an eagerness on the part of the English to court American sympathy.

Although Americans who loved peace for peace's sake or peace with England from racial loyalty were numerous enough to raise an impressive voice in December, 1895, they were far less audible than the aggressive patriots during the early months

of the year. The want of spirit in Cleveland's conduct of foreign relations was under attack from many quarters.

Republican politicians and editors led the charge. They resented deeply the rebuke to them inherent in Cleveland's Hawaiian policy; they hated Gresham as a renegade Republican. Moreover, they had long ago branded the President's tariff views as subservience to Britain and free trade. The brilliant and caustic Lodge was probably the most formidable critic of Democratic foreign policy, but Senators Cullom of Illinois and Chandler of New Hampshire were equally partisan and outspoken. Young Theodore Roosevelt was using all his growing influence to rout the pacifists. He paid his compliments to anti-imperialists like Edward Atkinson in these words:

These solemn prattlers strive after an ideal in which they shall happily unite the imagination of a green grocer with the heart of a Bengalese baboo. They are utterly incapable of feeling one thrill of generous emotion, or the slightest throb of that pulse which gives to the world statesmen, patriots, warriors, and poets, and which makes a nation other than a cumberer of the world's surface.

If the Democrats had supported the pacific policies of the administration as vigorously as the Republicans attacked them, the State Department might have ignored its critics. But the Republicans had the satisfaction of knowing that their dislike of Clevelandism in foreign affairs was shared in important sections of the Democratic party.

The Democratic chairman of the Senate Foreign Relations Committee, John T. Morgan of Alabama, was completely out of sympathy with Cleveland and Gresham. He was hostile to Cleveland's foreign policy not only because he favored the annexation of Hawaii and more activity in promoting the Isthmian canal, but because he was a silverite. All the silver enthusiasts—Democratic as well as Republican and Populist—portrayed Cleveland's monetary policies as being in the interest of English money lords. Jingoism and hostility to England were integral parts of silver oratory.

The American Irish were another group disturbed by charges that the Cleveland administration was pro-British. Events during the last decade had served to make Irish dislike of England an important political factor. The long-standing alliance of the Irish-Americans with the Democratic party had been challenged throughout the eighties by a persistent effort of the Republicans to woo them away. It had required energetic organization on the Democratic side to hold the Irish in line for Cleveland in 1892. Practical Democratic politicians still lived in fear that the Republicans might achieve the reputation of being the more valiant defenders of the eagle over the lion.

Peace advocates and jingoes were competing for the ear of the American public in the early months of 1895. By the testimony of all observers, whatever their own prepossession, it was the jingoes who made their appeal the more effectively. It became common opinion that there was something "un-American" about the spiritless conduct of foreign affairs by the Cleveland administration.

In almost every issue on which jingoes and anti-jingoes clashed, Anglo-American relations were involved. When American expansionists agitated for the annexation of Hawaii, it was asserted that Great Britain was about to seize it; when the same group advocated a great navy, America was menaced by British naval supremacy; when they demanded an American-controlled Isthmian canal, England was intending to dominate the proposed waterway. Editorial writers, like politicians, found baiting England easy and popular. A secretary in the British embassy in Washington wrote that it would be "a comfort to go to a country where one can read the news without finding in every paper an article accusing one's country of every conceivable crime."

It was in such an atmosphere that American policy on the Venezuelan question was being formulated. The situation had not caused much popular agitation until March, 1895. Neither Cleveland's advocacy of arbitration of the dispute in his annual message of December, 1894, nor the passage of a congressional resolution to the same effect in February had occasioned any considerable comment. Immediately after the adjournment of Congress, however, newspaper references to the dispute became increasingly frequent. In part this was simply a phase of the general jingo campaign against Cleveland, but ammunition for these particular volleys was supplied by active friends of Venezuela. William L. Scruggs, who had been United States minister to Venezuela under Harrison, was now a special agent of the Venezuelan government and active propagandist. The preceding fall he had written a pamphlet entitled "British Aggressions in Venezuela, or the Monroe Doctrine on Trial." It was sold on newsstands and distributed gratis and generously to editors and politicians. In March another pamphlet, prepared by E. R. Johnes "of counsel" for the Venezuelan government, was making its way into the hands of editors. Other less open influences were doubtless at work. Spring Rice complained: "The South Americans are in with all the low press men and every sort of lie is propagated about British aggression." Mrs. Gresham in the biography of her husband refers to the activities of speculators, and Bayard in London was alarmed at reports of the manipulations of American concessionaires.

The jingo press accepted without question the Venezuelan view of the issue.

To the New York *Tribune* the case was "perfectly simple." Venezuela owned the land; Great Britain coveted it and was trying to grab it—by guile if she could, by force if she must. The New York *Sun* declared that, should the Venezuelans be forced to fight for their rights, it would become the duty of American citizens to support them. Inaccurate accounts that Bayard had reported a refusal of the British to arbitrate were handled by even the more peaceful papers in a way likely to irritate American opinion. "None Of Our Business" was the headline summary of the British position as seen by the Boston *Transcript*, while the New York *World*, which was to win great prestige as a peacemaker in December, was indulging in extremely provocative headlines in April.

The English, however, failed to heed the danger signals which warned of rising American temper. Just when the Venezuelan issue was approaching a crisis, the British foreign office proceeded to take drastic action against Nicaragua and thus arouse a new tempest of American protest. News of a British ultimatum to this Central American state became public in March, and from then on until the final settlement of the affair in May the newspapers kept the matter almost constantly on the first page under sensational headlines.

Diplomatically the "Corinto affair," as the incident came to be called, was not very important. The British government demanded reparation from Nicaragua for the seizure and expulsion from the latter's territory of several British subjects, including a consular agent. At the expiration of the three-month period set for compliance with these demands, British men-of-war proceeded to Nicaraguan waters, and on April 27 British marines occupied the port of Corinto. On May 2 a settlement was announced accepting the guarantee of Salvador for the payment of the required in-

demnity, and British evacuation followed promptly. The Cleveland administration handled the matter cautiously. Asked by Nicaragua to intervene against an alleged violation of the Monroe Doctrine, Gresham held that the doctrine was not involved so long as Great Britain evidenced no purpose of permanently occupying American soil. However, the good offices of the United States were used, first, in an attempt to secure a further period of grace for Nicaragua before the occupation of Corinto, and then in smoothing the way for the eventual settlement.

The citizen who learned of these events through the daily press found them presented as much more exciting than they really were. Our Atlantic fleet was cruising in the Caribbean, and every movement of the ships was interpreted as being related to the Nicaraguan affair. Official denials that any special significance was to be attributed to these maneuvers served only to whet popular interest. News dispatches also reported great activity at the State Department, where Gresham was said to have notified the British government that coercive action against Nicaragua would be considered an infraction of the Monroe Doctrine.

Having reported that the administration's policy was much more active than it really was, the jingo press then made much of what it portrayed as a backdown by Cleveland and Gresham. "We Will Not Protest," said the New York *Sun* headlines, "England May Land Troops In Nicaragua For All Of Us." The actual occupation of Corinto brought to a head all the hostile criticism of the President. Editorial writers doubted the assurances of Great Britain that no permanent acquisition of territory was contemplated. "All the world knows what a temporary occupation by Great Britain means," asserted the Boston *Post*, while the Philadelphia *Press* declared:

"What is the most amazing and embittering is that this act of British aggression is consummated with the assent and sanction of the American Administration."

The politicians were even more severe than the press in denunciation of Cleveland's policy. Legislative houses in Missouri, Connecticut, and New York passed resolutions condemning what the New York assembly termed "the supineness, dilatoriness and lack of National and patriotic spirit which has characterized the Administration in dealing with this complication." Particularly serious for the administration were pronouncements by leading senators. Shelby Cullom, ranking Republican member of the Foreign Relations Committee, was quoted as saying: "If a plain, emphatic protest had been made by the United States Government, England would not have occupied Corinto. Now that she is there, I believe in using force, if necessary, to get her out." Senator Morgan vehemently denounced British policy and asserted that Congress would deal with these aggressions in its next session. A bitterly sarcastic open letter was directed to the President by Senator Stewart of Nevada. Cleveland was congratulated for his "conspicuous bravery in promoting the policy of the mother country," not only in exterminating "obnoxious bimetallists and pestiferous farmers" opposed to British financial policy but in co-operating cordially "in the policy of conquest and dominion for the mother country."

The excesses of the jingoes did not pass entirely without rebuke. Senator Hill of New York warned against adventurous and unwarranted applications of the Monroe Doctrine, while many newspapers denied that American interests were threatened by the events in Nicaragua. The State Department itself attempted a modest bit of civic education by putting out a pamphlet containing the exact words of President Monroe in an attempt to demonstrate the inapplicability of the famous doctrine to this controversy.

The eventual withdrawal of the British seemed to the moderates proof that the administration's policy had been justified. In a note to Gresham the President wrote: "I suppose you hear how matters are straightening out in our foreign relations. Our turn to feel well is at hand and the 'jingoes' are hunting for good back seats." The Boston *Transcript* hailed another defeat for the "congressional blatherskites" who were attempting to excite war fever against Great Britain.

Criticism of Cleveland and Gresham did not, however, abate in the least. Headlines in the *Tribune* were bitter, and the Toledo *Blade* asserted: "Had James G. Blaine been Secretary of State the past year, Americans would not now be hanging their heads in shame and humiliation." Comments in the British press as quoted in American newspapers were such as to add to Cleveland's difficulties. On the one side, praise for American neutrality in a tone described as "unctuous adulation" lent color to charges that the President was pro-British. On the other hand, some English comment was dangerously provocative. The London *Daily Graphic* called Nicaragua a "martyr to Monroeism" who was being given a "lesson long needed" by Latin America. The London *Globe* rejoiced that a "sharp little lesson" had been given not only to Nicaragua but also to the United States, whose disposition to interfere in disputes between smaller states and Europe was as "objectionable" as it was "uncalled for."

The Corinto affair, trivial as a diplomatic incident, is essential to an understanding of the background of the Venezuelan policy. Whether or not we had any right to intervene, large sections of the public did not like Great Britain's heavy-handed method in dealing with a small American state. The Cleveland administration had to take a severe drubbing, and the experience unquestionably influenced its subsequent dealings with England.

Evidences of increasing discontent with Cleveland's foreign policy were to be found in the rank and file of the Democratic party. "The Old Guard of the Democracy," said the *Sun*, "has been completely demoralized and estranged by the surrender of American interests." In a meeting of the Connecticut Democratic State Committee the blunt assertion was made that the Democrats of that state did not approve the President's foreign policy. The principal speaker at the annual meeting of the Interstate Democratic Association of the District of Columbia called for the maintenance of the Monroe Doctrine, which, it was asserted, the British admiral at Corinto had called "an obsolete doctrine" and a "myth."

Democrats close to the administration shared this impatience with conservatism in diplomacy. William C. Whitney cabled from Italy to commend Gresham for an unexpected display of vigor. Before the American Society in London our ambassador to France, James Eustis, indulged in fulsome praise of the United States, which, he said, had great strength but never used it for the oppression of small nations. The *Tribune* and the *Sun* contrasted the patriotic Eustis with Bayard, who—*horribile dictu*—had proposed a toast to Queen Victoria at the same banquet.

The most notable incident, however, indicating the desire of the Cleveland Democrats to assert their own lusty patriotism was the speech of Don M. Dickinson on May 10. Dickinson was a close friend of Cleveland and had been Postmaster General in his first administration. At a banquet of the Loyal Legion in Detroit he spoke to the provocative toast, "Our Veterans: Can They Hear the Bugle Call?" The hope that the age of wars was past, he said, did not square with the evidence of European imperialism and militarism. He called for a stronger American navy and related the history of England's long hostility to the United States, laying particular stress on Britain's "most extraordinary claims and movements" in Nicaragua and Venezuela.

Dickinson's speech was widely reported. Many papers assumed that it was intended as a rebuke to Cleveland and Gresham. A few observed the more suggestive fact that it was delivered directly after a trip to Washington on which Dickinson had visited the President and that it probably reflected a growing concern on the part of the administration with the reproaches against its Americanism.

The anxiety of Cleveland over the Venezuelan issue was further evidenced by the fact that the President personally canvassed the field for an exceptional man to assume the duties of minister to Venezuela. The position was offered in turn to ex-Governor Russell of Massachusetts, to G. L. Rives of New York, and to John Bassett Moore. Cleveland was apparently still thinking in terms of a cautious policy, because all of these men were prominent critics of the jingoes. Moore had just published a pamphlet on the Monroe Doctrine in which the historic document was very conservatively construed.

Secretary Gresham, meanwhile, was working long hours over the draft of a new note to Great Britain on the boundary dispute. According to his wife, the Secretary was confident that the difficulty could yet be settled without friction, that he could present such a statement of the facts that the British government would accept arbitration. It is probable, however, that not all the cabinet were content with so cautious a policy. When Gresham became seriously ill, the persistent Scruggs went directly to the President with an appeal for strong action.

On May 28 death removed Gresham from the perplexities of the State Department. The naming of Richard Olney as his successor was interpreted at once as evidence that the President intended to pursue a more vigorous foreign policy. This was due in part to Olney's reputation for decisive action gained in the Chicago strike crisis but more particularly to reports that the Attorney General had been a conspicuous advocate of firmer diplomacy in recent Cabinet meetings. Most significant of all, it was known that Olney had already been working on the Venezuelan case before the death of Gresham. The New York *Tribune* asserted at once that a new departure in foreign policy was impending. Scruggs responded to the change of personnel in the State Department by sending Olney a copy of his famous pamphlet and a fulsome letter in which the publicist expressed "every confidence in your ability and purpose to make the American name respected abroad".

The determination to stiffen American policy, apparent when Olney took over the State Department, must have been increased by the clear signs that the Republicans were seeking to gain further advantage from the situation. In June the Republican Club of New York City was giving publicity to a report dilating on the British invasion of Nicaragua and the Monroe Doctrine. In June, also, appeared an important magazine article on the Venezuelan question written by Senator Lodge. He intended it to pave the way for a stiff declaration of the Monroe Doctrine by the next Congress. It would "make some of the brethren sit up and take notice."

To Olney and Cleveland, now preparing to take a firm line, one of the most troublesome obstacles was the attitude of Ambassador Bayard. A low opinion of the Spanish-Americans, a fear of the pressure of speculators, a dislike of jingoism, plus what the *Tribune* called a lack of "the superb and indispensable quality of making himself disagreeable at the proper time" had made Bayard overcautious in the conduct of negotiations on the Venezuelan matter. Even a subordinate in the London embassy was grumbling about him. On June 22 J. R. Roosevelt wrote to Secretary Lamont:

> Mr. Bayard has gone off for a month and I am in charge. He is as good and nice and charming as ever, but sometimes I can't help wishing that we had a little more backbone here. I try hard to get it, but of course I only get sat down upon!! He read Lodge's article and was very angry about it and of course Lodge does make himself ridiculous. But I am certain our English cousins think more of us if we hold up *well* our own end of the line, and don't pat them on the back too much.

Olney's problem, then, was to strengthen American policy, to offset Bayard's lack of vigor, and also to compose a document which would, when eventually published, clear the administration of its reputation for lack of Americanism. The fruit of the Secretary's labors was the famous note of July 20. The logical and historical shortcomings of Olney's dispatch have since been laid bare by able scholars, but the President was much pleased with his Secretary's handiwork. It is possible that Cleveland was as enthusiastic over the prospect of scoring points over his domestic critics as over Lord Salisbury. He wrote to Dickinson: "In due time it will be found that the Administration has not been asleep. The devils that were cast out of the swine centuries ago have, I am afraid, obtained possession of some so-called Democratic leaders."

Olney's dispatch was composed and sent with the utmost secrecy. Even in the State Department only a very few individuals knew what was happening, and every effort was made to keep the press in the dark. Cleveland and Olney obviously hoped that by pressing their case vigorously they would achieve something concrete which could be presented to Congress in December—thus heading off an almost certain political field day on foreign affairs. While the new policy was in gestation, there was for a time a lull in the public discussion of the boundary dispute.

By October, however, a new discussion of the Venezuelan dispute had broken forth in the newspapers—much to the annoyance of Cleveland, who blamed leaks in the State Department. Both English and American journalists were excited by reports that the United States had sent Great Britain a ninety-day ultimatum. The *St. James Gazette* said: "Isn't it awful? But it might be still more awful if we only knew what the blessed Monroe Doctrine was, or what on earth the United States government has got to do with a quarrel between Great Britain and another independent state." The New York *World* doubted that the diplomats had sent an ultimatum, but "the people have prepared an ultimatum and are ready to enforce it. It is that England shall never control the mouth of the Orinoco or any other American river south of the Canadian line." The British position seemed absurd to even conservative papers like the Boston *Evening Transcript*, which thus summarized the English case: "Great Britain, having helped herself to a large slice of Venezuelan territory, will submit to arbitration whether she shall have any more."

Long before Salisbury's reply to Olney was ready, the British government took action which the press was quick to interpret as being the real answer to American intervention. First came alarming reports of military preparations being carried out in British Guiana under direct order of Joseph Chamberlain, then colonial

secretary in the British government. Still more inflammatory was the news that the British government was planning to repeat the tactics tried out in Nicaragua. A three-month ultimatum was being sent to Venezuela demanding an apology and compensation for the arrest of British subjects within the disputed territory.

It was this cool proposal to regard the boundary dispute as a closed matter and to proceed to the punishment of Venezuela on another issue that provoked more heated comment than had yet appeared in the controversy. Front-page headlines in the New York *Tribune* characterized the ultimatum as "A Direct Slap In The Face." The New Orleans *Picayune* regarded the action of Great Britain as "nothing more than an attempt to extend her territory in South America" and asserted that "the demands of the Monroe Doctrine will receive no attention from Great Britain unless we are prepared to back up our position by a show of force."

English newspaper comment was scarcely less provocative. "Lord Salisbury's ultimatum," proclaimed the *Times*, "has not come a moment too soon." The *Westminster Gazette* thought that "Venezuela, like Nicaragua, after much fuss, will probably prove to be small beer." The *St. James Gazette* was, as usual, the spokesman for the most offensive brand of British imperialism. After a reference to the Monroe Doctrine as a "blessed Mesopotamia" it said: "It would become the position of the United States as a great civilized Power much better to join us in bringing these Spanish-Indian barbarians to order."

Politicians exploited the issue for all it was worth. Theodore Roosevelt was having "fun" making jingo speeches, while in England, where he was traveling, Senator Lodge expressed strong views to both American and British reporters. Senator Chandler wrote an editorial for his own

Concord (New Hampshire) *Evening Monitor* entitled "Our Coming War with England—A Prediction." Congressmen Joseph Wheeler of Alabama and Charles H. Grosvenor of Ohio discussed "Our Duty in the Venezuelan Crisis" in the *North American Review*, while in the same magazine Lieutenant Governor Charles T. Saxton of New York wrote that the great majority of Americans felt "humiliated beyond expression" by the foreign policy of the administration. Cleveland's weakness in asserting the Monroe Doctrine was further denounced by Governor D. H. Hastings of Pennsylvania before a great Republican rally in New York City.

Prominent Democrats, who were dismayed at the attempt of the Republicans to set up a monopoly in patriotism, urged Cleveland and Olney to be vigorous. A few state elections were being held in November, 1895, and, more important, a presidential campaign was close at hand. William C. Whitney advised Secretary Herbert that Olney was "in a position to bring himself strongly to the front if he would only take a strong stand for the Monroe Doctrine in the matter of Venezuela." To Olney himself Whitney wrote: "All the State Department has needed for a long time was a strong man . . . who was not afraid to resist the encroachment of the European powers over here."

From local Democratic politicians, also, came a stream of advice. Olney was assured that the rank and file of the party strongly favored a vigorous enforcement of the Monroe Doctrine. A party worker in Maryland attributed Democratic defeats in that state to "the Monroe Doctrine" and appealed for ammunition to use against the jingoes. An Irish officeholder in Boston begged Olney not to let a Democratic administration permit England to "steal any part of this hemisphere." Congressman Ikirt of Ohio wrote that "a little Jingo"

would help in electing a friend. From Wisconsin came advice to call every bluff, and the people "will see you through the woods if it takes all winter and all the surplus in the Treasury." Most outspoken of all was the counsel of Congressman Thomas M. Paschal of Texas. The Venezuelan issue, he said, was a "winner" from every angle—especially to knock the pus out of the "anarchistic, socialistic & populistic boil." Furthermore, a foreign war would help in the assimilation of the "vast stream of immigration that has been pouring in and diffusing itself over the country."

As November slipped away, the impatience of Cleveland and Olney with the failure of Lord Salisbury to reply to the July note increased. For months it had been apparent that the opening of Congress would force a showdown on foreign policy. Morgan, Stewart, Cullom, Chandler, and Lodge had in effect announced their intention of precipitating a bitter debate. Moreover, for months reports had been allowed to circulate unchallenged that the administration was actually taking a strong line in the Venezuelan matter. The supporters of Cleveland expected that the annual message would provide a vindication for the President's policy; his enemies anticipated a revelation of his failure.

Ambassador Bayard, however, continued to pursue extremely cautious tactics. He had not found an opportunity to deliver Olney's note to Lord Salisbury until August 7. His report of the interview referred to a previous minister's "uncertainty as to the wisdom or expediency of renewing our recommendations for a settlement by arbitration between the two Powers" and expressed a desire to keep such questions "in the atmosphere of serene and elevated effort." Bayard's lack of enthusiasm for the Olney policy was evident also in a letter to Cleveland in which he asserted: "The principles involved are serious—and the facts complicated—as necessarily must be the case where responsibility for the acts and rights of an independent third party is assumed." In October he wrote Olney that he was indisposed to express his anxiety to secure a reply from the British foreign office. As late as November 23 he reported: "The circumstances which have caused delay are not doubtful and it would be unjust to suppose that it has arisen from any other than involuntary obstructions." The failure of Lord Salisbury's reply to arrive in Washington before the delivery of the annual message was a most unfortunate added irritant to Anglo-American friction. Although this delay was largely caused by a stupid misunderstanding in the British foreign office as to the date of the opening of Congress, it seems probable that Bayard did little to impress the British government with the urgency of the situation.

The President could only refer in his regular message to the acute stage into which the dispute between Great Britain and Venezuela had passed and assure the legislators that the United States had taken a firm position based on the Monore Doctrine and was waiting for a British reply. There was something of anticlimax in this, and a curiously mixed response resulted from the country. On December 4 the New York *Tribune* was complimenting the President on his commitment to the "identical program which *The Tribune* first outlined," but two days later the same paper was pouring scorn on Cleveland for "Begging an Answer." Some letters coming to the President's desk praised him for asserting the Monroe Doctrine, others for resisting the tide of jingoism.

It was commonly assumed that Congress would take some action. The Chicago *Inter-Ocean* declared: "The people are now more importunate in the demand for a more American foreign policy than

anything else. It is the latest of popular demands and this Congress is sure to heed it." It is evident that Cleveland considered the legislators as the factor in the situation most likely to force action. When he left Washington for a brief hunting trip, he directed Olney to put Salisbury's reply, if it arrived, into his pocket "so that no one will know that you have it until I return. . . .If I were here, I would not be hurried in the matter even if the Congress should begin grinding again the resolution-of-inquiry mill."   .

Not one, but several, congressional mills began to grind at once. Lodge introduced a resolution affirming the Monroe Doctrine—much to the delight of Theodore Roosevelt. Senator Cullom introduced a similar resolution and spoke for an hour in its support. Senator Morgan attacked England in a two-hour speech reviewing the Bering Sea controversy. Ambassador Bayard was raked over the coals in the House on an issue unrelated to the boundary dispute but with an animosity due in part, no doubt, to the unpopularity of his reputed Anglophilism. Most interesting maneuver of all was a resolution offered by Representative Livingston of Georgia. He proposed the creation of a joint congressional committee to examine into the facts connected with the Venezuelan dispute and to recommend a course of action. To reporters Livingston explained that such a committee could sit in the United States and that he had in his own possession all the necessary data for a thorough investigation. In case Great Britain refused to renounce territory held in violation of Venezuela's rights, the representative claimed that all the Democrats and two thirds of the Republicans in the House would favor declaring war. Livingston may not have been a bad judge of congressional sentiment on the issue; he had been the author of the resolution on Venezuela which had passed Congress in the spring without a dissenting vote.

The leadership which Congress might have assumed was, however, taken by the administration. The sequence of events is well known. Salisbury's reply—imposing in its dialectic but very irritating in tone—at length arrived. Cleveland returned from his hunting, and the stout special message was composed and sent to Congress. The tumultuous response in Congress and in the country at large may be attributed less to the emotion-raising potency of the President's phrases than to the fact that he seemed at last to be marching in time with the martial music which had been stirring American spirits.

It would be inconsistent with the character of Cleveland to conclude that the famous message was motivated either by the demogogic seizure of a popular issue or by a surrender to political pressure. Courage, honesty, and a sense of duty were basic qualities with the President, and he challenged England on the Venezuelan issue only after he became personally convinced that the Monroe Doctrine was at stake and that it was his duty to maintain it.

Nevertheless, no statesman, however independent, can isolate himself from the prevailing spirit of his times. It was the agitation of the issue by politicians and journalists which must explain both the seriousness with which the administration came to consider a distant boundary dispute and also the aggressive tone which the Olney note and the Cleveland message displayed. In reality a crisis existed independently of the action of the President. It grew out of the insistent demand of influential groups that the United States intervene in the Venezuelan situation. Had Cleveland failed to act and had hostilities arisen between Venezuela and England, a much worse situation than the December crisis might have resulted. Any prolonged

struggle would have created a state of affairs perilously like that which involved us in war in 1898. It is, in fact, as evidence of the rising tide of aggressive American nationalism that the Venezuelan crisis is most interesting. A friend of Cleveland thus described the atmosphere of 1895:

The mere political situation need not alarm us, but we have to do with that most mysterious, most reasonless, yet most constant and controlling force in public affairs: that of periods or cycles. Not the mere wobbling from election to election, but something of longer range and deeper source. I note that it was just thirty years from the end of the Revolution to the beginning of the war of 1812, and just thirty years from the end of that war to the beginning of the Mexican. Neither of these last wars was necessary and they were repugnant to a large, respectable portion of the population. But the time had come around for a fight. It is now thirty years, the length of a generation, since the great Civil War. Most Americans now living remember nothing of it. Vaguely and uneasily that part of the beast in man appears to be rousing in our country. How came it in? How comes the sea in? The proofs are nowhere, the signs are everywhere.

Despite the dangerous state of American feeling no war with England resulted. Various factors contributed to insure a peaceful settlement. In the first place, it should be remarked that, belligerent though Cleveland and Olney had been, their desire and purpose was peace. It is possible that even the wording of Olney's note and his own special message seemed less strong to the President than to others. This was often true of the language which Cleveland used. At all events, Cleveland's action in December furnished the opportunity for all peaceloving elements to assert themselves. A major portion of the British public at once demanded some settlement other than war, while in the United States pressure for a peaceful solution, although not so nearly universal, was very strong in certain localities and among certain influential professions—in New York and Boston, for example, and among businessmen, educators, and the clergy. Lord Salisbury and Joseph Chamberlain were as little desirous of allowing the controversy to proceed to a violent end as were Cleveland and Olney. Particularly after the Jameson raid and the Kruger telegram the danger of England's isolation and the reality of Germany's hostility were patent. Step by step the British government retreated from the position taken in Lord Salisbury's note. At length the consent of all parties was obtained for the settlement of the boundary dispute by an international arbitration with the proviso that occupation of territory for fifty years by either Venezuela or Great Britain should be judged to constitute title. Although the final decision of the arbitral body failed to recognize the extreme Venezuelan claims which American editors had been championing, opinion in this country was generally satisfied. England has been successfully challenged and induced to recognize the special position of the United States in the Americas. This pleased our nationalists, who were, after all, not primarily interested in just where the vagrant Venezuelan boundary finally came to rest.

WALTER LaFEBER (1933-   ), professor of history at
Cornell University, is intrigued by the same question that
perplexes most scholars who study Grover Cleveland: why
did Cleveland respond to the Venezuelan boundary
dispute in such belligerent tones? Suggesting that
Cleveland wanted to promote American economic interests
in the area, LaFeber imputes much more coherence and
rationality to the President's action than have most
scholars. But assuming that LaFeber's explanation for
Cleveland's policy is adequate, we still must evaluate the
wisdom of the policy. And to do this, we must attempt to
answer the same kind of question which faced Cleveland
and Olney: would an extension of Britain's influence into
Latin America have made it more difficult for the United
States to expand economically into the area?*

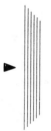

► *The Need for Foreign Markets*

The policy that Grover Cleveland's
second administration formulated in the
Venezuelan controversy of 1895-1896 was a
direct answer to British encroachments on
United States interests in Latin America.
Political and business leaders believed
these American interests to be economic,
strategic, and political. The economic influence on the shaping of Cleveland's
policy in this dispute has not received sufficient attention. After the 1893 depression
paralyzed the domestic economy, United
States attention focused increasingly on
Latin America; indeed, it is significant that
the controversy occurred during the depths
of that business crisis.

American interests, both economic and
strategic, were threatened during the 1893-

1895 period by ominous British moves in
Brazil, Nicaragua, the disputed area in
Venezuela itself, and the small island of
Trinidad off the Brazilian coast. During the
same years Germany and France menaced
United States advantages in Brazil and the
Caribbean. Gravely concerned, the State
Department finally forced a showdown
struggle on the issue of the Venezuelan
boundary. By successfully limiting British
claims in this incident, the United States
won explicit recognition of its dominant
position in the Western Hemisphere.

This essay attempts to trace two developments: that international dangers motivated the Cleveland administration in for-
mulating the Venzuelan policy; that the
economic crisis arising out of the 1893 de-

*Reprinted from Walter LaFeber, "The Background of Cleveland's Venezuelan Policy: A Reinterpre-
tation," *American Historical Review*, LXVI (July, 1961), 947-967. Footnotes omitted.

pression provided the context and played an important role in this policy formulation. This is not to say that the economic influence was the only motivating force, but that this factor, relatively overlooked by previous writers on the subject, greatly shaped the thinking of both the Cleveland administration and key segments of American society.

Five considerations should serve to establish the validity of this interpretation: timing played a key role in that the year 1895 witnessed a convergence of forces which brought the United States into the controvery (after the argument had simmered over half a century) and led it to assert control over the nations of the Western Hemisphere; the Cleveland administration and the American business community viewed foreign markets, especially those of Latin America, as providing a solution to the domestic depression; policy makers in Washington believed the Monroe Doctrine to be important primarily for what Secretary of State Richard Olney called its "practical benefits," that is, its potential strategic and economic benefits; the State Department acted unilaterally in the affair, cared little for Venezuelan opinion or advice, and hoped to benefit American interests primarily, not Venezuelan; neither the political situation in the United States nor the newly discovered "psychic crisis" of the 1890's played important roles in key American decisions.

The events leading to the Venezuelan crisis were silhouetted against the somber and ominous background of the 1893-1897 depression. Economic crisis had threatened the United States since 1890 and 1891, when only unexampled American exports had averted financial trouble. Despite these huge exports, American prices and wages continued their long downward swing which had begun in 1873. By late

1892 and early 1893 business observers recognized that the American economic system had reached a point of maturity which disrupted its relations with the markets of the world. Panic struck the weakened nation in the spring of 1893 when the Philadelphia and Reading Railroad and the National Cordage Company collapsed.

Political and social uprisings, which were renewed and intensified by the economic breakdown, forced the Cleveland administration not only to face the problem of reviving a glutted industrial system, but to do so before radical politcal forces paralyzed the administration's initiative. Labor unrest manifested itself in the marches of Coxey's and Hogan's armies of the unemployed on Washington—marches which highly dramatized the fact that the great American frontier no longer attracted, but even repelled the discontented of the nation—and in the nearly successful attempt of the socialist wing of the American Federation of Labor to control that body. The threat posed by restless farmers (and many businessmen) in the West and South compounded the danger of labor dissatisfaction. Among others, James J. Hill and the assistant chairman of the Kansas State Democratic Committee warned Cleveland in 1893 that all the "isms" that had plagued society in the past were "now appearing in an organized and most formidable manner."

Cleveland quickly reacted by calling a special session of Congress to repeal the Silver Purchase Act of 1890. The President hoped that the repeal would stabilize the country on a gold standard. Though this action had little immediate effect on the economy, the administrations' reasons for the repeal pointed the way for further ameliorative action. Cleveland and his advisers assumed that the economic problems stemmed not from the lack of circulating medium (as the Populists and silverites charged), but from bad monetary laws and overproduction. Since a powerful Populist-silver bloc in Congress could sidetrack any legislation that would carefully regulate and restrict the amount of paper money, the administration emphasized overproduction as the causative factor of the depression. This, in turn, led to a quest for foreign markets.

In a speech to the New York Chamber of Commerce in November 1893, Secretary of the Treasury John G. Carlisle explained the administration's belief that the gold standard and an expanded foreign trade went hand in hand. Carlisle declared that "our commercial interests are not confined to our own country; they extend to every quarter of the globe, and our people buy and sell in nearly every market of the civilized world. . . . Without exception these prices are fixed in the markets of countries having a gold standard." Carlisle's *Annual Reports* and many of Cleveland's public statements emphasized the administration's belief that foreign trade provided a key to America's economic revival and that the gold standard was necessary for such trade.

Two other developments motivated the Cleveland administration to view enlarged foreign trade as a means to end the depression: the withdrawal of British investments and the closing of the American frontier. American political and business leaders believed the exodus of British capital from the United States to be a basic cause of the panic. When the repeal of the Silver Purchase Act failed to attract new foreign investments, the administration and the business community turned to the hope of a large foreign trade surplus as a replacement for the withdrawn capital. Such a trade balance would not only provide fresh capital to invigorate stagnant American industries, but newly found markets would revive these industries to a point where they would again be appealing to outside investors.

Cleveland and others in influential positions coupled this view of foreign capital with the belief that a mature American system had finally absorbed its western frontier. They viewed this occurrence with alarm. Cleveland made special mention of this in his annual message in 1893 and later attempted to reopen western lands that had been claimed by speculators. Obviously, if the closed frontier had been a leading cause in the glutting of the home market, the Republican protective tariff had to be revised. The Democrats thus proposed a tariff that they believed would stimulate the movement of domestic surpluses into world markets.

In this desire to reinvigorate production instead of redistributing goods, Cleveland asked for a tariff bill that would include a long list of free raw materials. He believed that if these industrial essentials entered the United States tariff-free, "the world [would] be open to our national ingenuity and enterprise." He related this hope of world markets to the growing labor unrest by noting that "the limited demand for. . . goods" on a "narrow market" inevitably led to industrial stagnation. Carlisle expressed it more succinctly: "The demand for labor would steadily grow with the extension of trade."

Cleveland's two congressional leaders, William L. Wilson of West Virginia in the House and Roger Q. Mills of Texas in the Senate, shared these opinions. Wilson introduced the tariff by observing that it had been devised "in the shadow and depression of a great commercial crisis." He declared that the free raw materials clauses would lead to "the enlargement of markets for our products in other countries, the increase in the internal commerce and in the carrying trade of our own country." All these factors would "insure a growing home market." In effect, Wilson believed that the United States had to rebuild its home market by enlarging its foreign market. Mills echoed Wilson's statements, then added a new note by declaring that Great Britain would have to suffer economic setbacks since she blocked the path of America's economic manifest destiny. Mills believed that the British "saw with alarm the triumph of Mr. Cleveland as the representative of commercial expansion." Many other congressmen repeated these arguments during the tariff debates.

A group of protectionist senators gathered support to defeat the House bill and to substitute a quasi-protectionist measure of its own. This tariff measure resulted mainly from the lobbying of several trusts and from political and personal hatred for Cleveland. But during the congressional debate, the President continually reiterated the importance of the raw materials provisions. In disgust, he finally allowed the bill to become law without his signature, though only three free raw materials remained in the measure.

The American business community followed the example of the administration in attempting to devise new means of expanding its foreign commerce. The depression reached its deepest trough in 1894-1895 as exports, especially staple agricultural products, failed to revive the economy. Business circles recognized this condition and called for drastic measures. . . .

By late 1895 a concise economic analysis had led both the American business community and the administration to the conclusion that the United States industrial system needed more Latin American markets. Such a conclusion suggested that any expansion of European (especially British) influence in the area endangered not only America's security, but also its economic and political well-being.

In 1894 and 1895 these dynamic American policies clashed with expanding European claims in Brazil, Nicaragua, and Trinidad, a small island off the Brazilian coast. A revolution erupted in Brazil in September 1893. Rebels, led by promonarchist groups, hoped to end the four-year-old republic and restore the empire. But most important for American-Brazilian commercial relations, the insurgents included elements desiring to abrogate Brazil's reciprocity treaty with the United States— the most important one the United States possessed. The rebels planned to cut off all outside aid to the besieged government by blockading the harbor of Rio de Janeiro; indeed, they had placed all their hopes of success in this one embattled area. Secretary of State Gresham did little more in the early months of the revolution than promulgate the rule that American merchants and traders could continue their commerce with Rio harbor unless their ships crossed the line of fire.

Suddenly, in December 1893, the revolutionary cause grew stronger when a key Brazilian admiral, known for his promonarchist views, defected to the insurgents. Thus reinforced, the rebels announced that they would prevent all incoming trade from unloading in Rio harbor. This meant that all foreign ships would encounter "lines of fire." When German and British business interests endorsed the new rebel stand, the State Department feared that if the insurgent policy succeeded, American trading interests would lose their favored position. Influenced by urgent letters from United States exporters, especially Crossman Brothers of New York and Standard Oil President William Rockefeller, and guided by his own fervent belief that American industry needed more foreign markets, Gresham reversed his position in early January 1894. Sending a strong naval force to Rio harbor, the Secretary of State instructed the commander to protect with force the landing of American goods. This was accomplished, and the revolution collapsed. American congressional leaders, applauding Gresham's policy, portrayed Great Britain as the culprit in the rebellion. The republic had not only been saved from a monarchist-inspired plot, but United States commercial interests (as the American minister to Brazil was quick to point out) had preserved intact their private inroads into the Brazilian market. The German minister to Brazil remarked, "The American dollar started to roll in order to break off the monarchist point of the revolution."

Several months after the failure of this revolt, Gresham peacefully but firmly ejected British interests from the Mosquito Indian reservation in Nicaragua. This reservation occupied a crucial area, for it governed the eastern entrance to the proposed Nicaraguan canal. During the summer of 1894 the British hesitated leaving the region as they claimed that under an 1860 treaty they had obtained rights to protect the Indians from Nicaraguan injustices. Gresham disagreed and exerted continuous pressure on the British Foreign Office; in the fall of 1894 the British surrendered their position.

The American press disliked England's reluctance to leave this key area. When in the spring of 1895 British warships blockaded the Nicaraguan port of Corinto, American public and official opinion became aroused. An injury to a British citizen suffered during the 1894 trouble brought about the blockade. The State Department admitted the British right of blockade when it announced that the Monroe Doctrine had no relevance to the situation. But American press and business circles, concerned over the future safety of

an American-owned canal, deprecated the possibility that Great Britain would continue to rule over four million dollars worth of mushrooming American investment in bananas, timber, and inland trade in the reservation area. Gresham shared this alarm, for although he disavowed the pertinence of the Monroe Doctrine, he nevertheless expressed deep concern to American Ambassador Bayard in London. Then, with two strokes, the Secretary of State brought the reservation under United States control. First, Gresham implicitly agreed to protect the expanding American investments in the territory from Nicaraguan injustices. Second, he informed the British ambassador in Washington that henceforth the State Department would assume Britain's duties of guarding the rights of the mosquito Indians. By doing so, Gresham replaced England's control with that of the United States.

As Venezuelan matters moved to a climax in 1895, other British actions increased American apprehension. The Foreign Office attempted to force Nicaragua to reopen the delicate reservation problem. Though the outstanding points were soon settled, Alvey A. Adee, Second Assistant Secretary of State, told Olney that this irritation was "an important indication of the drift of British policy." England further worried Washington by occupying the island of Trinidad; it hoped to use this uninhabited jut of rock off the Brazilian coast as a cable station. The American press loudly supported Brazil's protests. Adee wrote Olney that "the newspaper men are wild about the Trinidad business." Under scrutiny of the State Department, Brazil and England reached an agreement in 1896.

Britain's multiplying claims in the Western Hemisphere caused Adee to exclaim to Olney in August 1895 that the British were playing a "grab game" throughout North and South America. But France also gave the State Department concern. In mid-1895 France and Venezuela severed relations over the French minister's alleged insult of the Venezuelan government. The United States stepped into the dispute and attempted to restore diplomatic connections. Bayard explained the State Department intervention when he wrote in August 1895 that the dispute was "of present interest" when viewed in "connection with the status of the existing Anglo-Venezuelan Boundary dispute.". . .

Congress and the Cleveland administration responded vigorously to these European encroachments. The character of this response can be briefly analyzed in the following incidents and personages: a congressional debate in the winter of 1894-1895 on the best means of protecting and expanding American commerce abroad; the naval appropriation debates of 1895 and 1896; a speech by Don Dickinson in May 1895; recognition by influential Americans that the Orinoco River was a vital pawn in the Venezuelan boundary dispute; Olney's concepts of American economic needs and power; statements of Cleveland and Olney during the Venezuelan boundary negotiations.

In the winter of 1894-1895 Congress became the center of an extended debate over American expansion into commercial and strategic areas and over the evolution of an anti-British policy. Henry Teller, leader of the Senate's silver bloc, sounded the keynote when he called England "our great commercial antagonist." Conservative Nelson Aldrich of Rhode Island concurred as he warned that "there is a commercial warfare. . .going on among the great nations of the world for enlarged markets" and added that the United States could not "sit down silently and submissively". . . .

During this and the 1895-1896 session, Congress passed naval appropriation measures that provided money for the continued construction of the new American battleship fleet. The first three battleships had been authorized in 1890, and another had been added in 1892. Congress accelerated the construction program in 1895 and 1896 when it authorized the construction of five more battleships. Significantly, Congress provided money to begin building these vessels even though the Treasury suffered from an acutely depressed condition.

The cry for both commercial expansion and protection against British encroachments appeared frequently in these naval debates. . . . By 1896 such arguments had silenced almost all previous opposition to the building of a battleship fleet.

Perhaps a speech delivered in May 1895 by Don Dickinson, a leader of the Democratic forces in Michigan and a close friend of President Cleveland, provided the most widely publicized commercial argument for American action in the Venezuelan dispute. One student of this episode calls Dickinson's speech "the most notable incident. . .indicating the desire of the Cleveland Democrats to assert their own lusty patriotism." It should be emphasized, however, that Dickinson's address was more than a reflection of internal political pressure on the Cleveland foreign policies. The speech was important because it symbolized a wide and strongly held opinion that the United States had to obtain additional foreign markets. In a flaming peroration that summarized the speech, Dickinson declared, "We need and must have open markets throughout the world to maintain and increase our prosperity." He realized that such American expansion would conflict with "the settled policy of Great Britain." Consequently, Dickinson asked that England's "extraordinary claims and movements" be watched closely in

Nicaragua and Venezuela. The President applauded the speech in a personal letter to Dickinson.

Cleveland had become interested in the Venezuelan dispute in early 1895, the importance of the Orinoco River especially attracting his attention. When Dickinson made a midnight call on the hard-working Chief Executive in April 1895, Cleveland displayed a large map showing the controversial boundary area. He explained that Great Britain had not previously formally included the mouth of the Orinoco in its territory, but recently the British Foreign Minister had entered such a claim. Cleveland expressed alarm since the control of the river meant the control of a rich section of the South American interior trade.

The State Department shared the President's concern, for it also realized the importance of the Orinoco for American commerce. In late 1894 Venezuela closed the river in an alleged effort to end smuggling. By quickly exerting diplomatic pressure to reopen the waterway, Gresham demonstrated that the United States valued the Orinoco. Venzuela took advantage of this incident to send a diplomatic note to Washington that stressed the dire consequences for American commerce if England gained control of the river's entrance. Then, on April 5, 1895, the British formally claimed the Orinoco's mouth. Between this date and May 25 events moved rapidly. Cleveland told Dickinson of his concern over the control of the river; Gresham asked Venezuela to restore diplomatic relations with England in order that the United States would "be in a position" to mediate; and the President began an urgent search to find "someone. . .of a much higher grade than is usually thought good enough" to send to the vacant ministerial post in Venezuela. Gresham finally began composing a long note on the subject which he planned

to send to Great Britain, but death cut short his task. Olney picked up and supercharged this growing American concern, then exploded it in the British Foreign Office with his note of July 20.

The real origins of the boundary dispute dated from 1841, but the United States entered the controversy much later, in 1883 and 1886, and then only briefly. The State Department made the British-Venezuelan controversy a three-cornered affair only toward the close of Gresham's term of office. Olney, former Attorney General, replaced Gresham upon the latter's death in May 1895. He possessed two beliefs that must be understood to comprehend American action in the dispute. First, he had a clear conception of the 1893 depression as a "labor revolution" which had resulted from the introduction of machine technology. With these new means of expanded production, more markets had to be found if Olney were to fulfill his hope of restraining this "revolution" to what he termed "peaceful and moderate channels." Second, he believed that the United States had emerged from its century of internal development as a full-fledged world power. The natural corollary of this was that the United States could now exert its will almost any place in the world, particularly in the Western Hemisphere. As Olney stated this concept, "It behooves us to accept the commanding position" the United States occupies "among the powers of the earth."

Olney embodied these beliefs in his July 20, 1895, note on the Venezuelan boundary question to British Prime Minister Lord Salisbury. The Secretary of State posited that American "honor and. . .interests" were involved in the controversy. He then tried to fit the Monroe Doctrine into the dispute. Historians might demonstrate that Olney made a poor fitting and that the doctrine, as defined by past use, did not apply to the question. This, however, does not lead to an understanding of either Olney's intentions or the aims of the Cleveland administration's foreign policy. Olney advanced the argument that American interests as well as Venezuelan territory were at stake. In essence, he interpreted the Monroe Doctrine as the catchall slogan that justified protecting America's self-interests. If the Monroe Doctrine had never existed, Olney's note would have been penned anyway; only the term "American self-interest" would have been substituted for the doctrine.

Declaring that the United States had political and commercial stakes in Latin America, the Secretary of State proceeded to proclaim the ideal of extending the American form of democracy to the world in sentences that resemble those of Wilson in 1917. He interrelated American interests with the Orinoco River since it controlled "the whole navigation of the interior of South America." Of vital significance is the context within which Olney placed these points, for he emphasized that the Monroe Doctrine was positive as well as negative. Not only did the doctrine formulate the rule of European abstinence from the Western Hemisphere, but "It aimed at also securing the practical benefits to result from the application of the rule." Olney then defined these benefits as "popular self-government" in Latin America, the commercial and political relationship of South and Central America to the United States, and the unencumbered use of the Orinoco. The Secretary of State climaxed this argument with the blunt assertion that if necessary these benefits could be secured and preserved by American force: "Today the United States is practically sovereign on this continent, and its fiat is law upon the subjects to which it confines its interposition."

When Lord Salisbury challenged these claims, Cleveland rephrased the American argument in his special message of December 17, 1895. The President first defined the Monroe Doctrine as a statement of self-interest. He then declared that the doctrine had to be maintained since it was "essential to the integrity of our free institutions and the tranquil maintenance of our distinctive form of government." Phrasing his message candidly, Cleveland warned that if Great Britain continued its course in the boundary dispute, the United States would regard this action "as a willful aggression upon its rights and interests."

The causes and intentions of the administration's policy are given in a personal letter from Cleveland to Bayard. The President emphasized two points. He wrote that the Monroe Doctrine had been invoked because of "its value and importance *to our government and welfare*, and that its defense and maintenance involve its application when a state of facts arises requiring it" [Cleveland's italics]. The President next strongly disclaimed any idea that internal political pressure, especially jingoism, had inspired the American action; such influence was "entirely irrelevant to the case and. . .had absolutely nothing to do with any action I have taken."

Throughout the ensuing negotiations, the United States acted unilaterally. Venezuela did not know that Olney had penned his July note until the newspapers printed the text. Even after this, the Cleveland administration did not consult Venezuela. When, in January 1896, Great Britain proposed a court of arbitration that included a Venezuelan representative, Olney countered with an offer excluding Venezuelan membership. The Secretary of State took the same position when he opposed including the Latin American nation in the negotiations. He argued that he did not care to have Venezuela "consulted at every step." Olney succeeded in including his plan for the court of arbitration in the treaty signed by England and the United States in November 1896. When the Caracas government learned of this, it demanded and obtained a representative on the tribunal. Even then Venezuela so intensely disliked both the treaty and the manner in which Olney had carried on negotiations that the legislature ratified the pact only after police ended threats of street rioting in Caracas.

The United States obtained its two principal objectives: England submitted the dispute to an arbitral commission, and in the final disposition Venezuela retained control of the Orinoco River. But most important, by submitting its case to arbitration, England recognized Olney's claim of American dominance in the Western Hemisphere.

American historians have offered three interpretations to explain the Cleveland administration's policy in the boundary dispute. The most popular explanation states that domestic political attacks "must explain both the seriousness with which the administration came to consider a distant boundary dispute and also the aggressive tone which the Olney note and the Cleveland message displayed." A second thesis traces the policy's roots to Olney's bellicose, stubborn temper. A third interpretation declares that a "psychic crisis" struck influential segments of American opinion in the 1890's and that a new spirit of manifest destiny emerged from this "crisis."

There can be little doubt that Cleveland took domestic political pressures into account, but defining these pressures as major causative elements leaves key questions unanswered and raises many others. Cleveland's bellicose policy could not have permanently won any political enemies to his side. The Republican jingoists and the

Democratic silver bloc led the cheering for the December 17 message. Neither of these groups would have agreed with Cleveland on national political objectives. The President actually alienated many of his strongest supporters, especially the eastern financiers who had once saved the gold reserve, and who, at Cleveland's request, repeated the rescue operation shortly after the December message. In other words, the administration's Venezuelan policy attracted groups that were irreconcilable in domestic politics, while repelling the administration's stanchest supporters. War might have united the nation behind him, but Cleveland certainly did not want to turn the controversy into an open conflict.

No reliable proof exists which shows that Cleveland hoped to benefit personally from the episode. It is extremely doubtful that with his conservative conception of the Chief Executive's duties and responsibilities he would have broken the third term tradition even if he had possessed the support. E. C. Benedict, who handled Cleveland's investments in stocks and bonds, testified three weeks before the Venezuelan message that the President had repeatedly said that he was "impatient" to end his term in office.

An interpretation that stresses Olney's bellicose character misses two important points. First, Gresham worked on a diplomatic note concerning the Venezuelan situation several months before Olney assumed the top position in the State Department. Second, Cleveland probably initiated the dispatch of the Olney note, reworked the draft, and heartily endorsed his Secretary of State's language. The President played an extremely important part in the formulation of the policy, especially during the crucial incubation period of April-July 1895.

A thesis which emphasizes that Cleveland bowed to the pressure of jingoism and a mass psychological need for vicarious excitement does an injustice to Cleveland. The President's greatest assets were his courage and a strong character. After all, Cleveland defied public pressures exerted for Hawaiian annexation, the application of the Monroe Doctrine in the Corinto dispute, and compromises in the silver repeal act and the 1894 tariff. There is no reason to believe that he suddenly bent to the winds of jingoism in 1895, unless he had better reasons than pleasing irreconcilable political enemies. It would be difficult, if not impossible, to put Cleveland and Olney in the social groups that supposedly were undergoing this psychological dilemma.

Olney and Cleveland acted as they did because they feared that United States interests were in jeopardy. Both men said this at the time, and there is no reason to doubt their word. Such danger emanated from actual or threatened European encroachments in Latin America. This expansion not only endangered both areas held vital for American strategic purposes and existing or possible political democracies in the Western Hemisphere, but it also threatened present and potential commercial markets for American products. Both the administration and the business community proclaimed these markets to be necessary for American economic and political health. They reasoned that increased shipments of industrial products to less developed regions would have to replace faltering agricultural products as the staple of American export trade; and, as a member of the State Department observed in 1895, "It has been the task of Mr. Cleveland's foreign policy to prepare the way" for these manufactured goods. One may speculate that Cleveland referred to both economic and security problems when he told a close friend late in 1896 that the Venezuelan affair was not a foreign question, but the "most distinct of home questions." As Olney realized, the mature power of the United States could be used to harvest what the Secretary of State called "the practical benefits" of the Monroe Doctrine. Then these "home questions" could be solved.

During the 1930s, when Gerald P. Nye and his Senate Munitions Investigating Committee suggested that American financiers and armament manufacturers dragged the United States into World War I, numerous intellectuals responded by suggesting that businessmen had been responsible for other wars. Reacting to such views, JULIUS W. PRATT, after extensive research, denied that American businessmen had been responsible for the Spanish-American War. Pratt's argument was so convincing that he and other historians began to explain the war in terms of mass hysteria, whipped up by yellow journalism and jingoists who acted from a variety of motives. Significantly, most historians used the implications of Pratt's study to absolve President McKinley of responsibility for manuevering the nation into war. In the process, they usually ended up demonstrating how McKinley was forced into a war against his will.°

The Business Point of View

We may begin with a generalization, the evidence for which will be presented as the chapter proceeds. American business, in general, had strongly opposed action that would lead to war with Spain. American business had been either opposed or indifferent to the expansionist philosophy which had arisen since 1890. But almost at the moment when war began, a large section of American business had, for reasons that will become apparent, been converted to the belief that a program of territorial expansion would serve is purposes. Hence business, in the end, welcomed the "large policy" and exerted its share of pressure for the retention of the Spanish islands and such related policies as the annexation of Hawaii and the construction of an isthmian canal.

One public man to whom the welfare of American business was of so much concern that he may almost be considered its spokesman in the Senate, was McKinley's friend, Mark Hanna. No one was more unwilling than he to see the United States drift into war with Spain. To Hanna, in the words of his biographer, "the outbreak of war seemed to imperil the whole policy of domestic economic amelioration which he placed before every other object of political action." Hanna's attitude appears to have been identical with that of leading business men. This conclusion is based not only upon the few published biographies of such

°Reprinted from Julius W. Pratt, *Expansionists of 1898* (Baltimore: The Johns Hopkins Press, 1938), pp. 233-257. Reprinted by permission of the publisher. Footnotes omitted.

men, but also upon the study of a large number of financial and trade periodials, of the proceedings of chambers of commerce and boards of trade, and of material in the *Miscellaneous Files* of the Department of State, containing numerous letters and petitions from business men and organizations.

That business sentiment, especially in the East, was strongly anti-war at the close of 1897 and in the opening months of 1898, is hardly open to doubt. Wall Street stocks turned downward whenever the day's news seemed to presage war and climbed again with information favorable to peace. Bulls and bears on the market were those who anticipated, respectively, a peaceable and a warlike solution of the Cuban question. The "jingo," in Congress or the press, was an object of intense dislike to the editors of business and financial journals, who sought to counteract his influence by anti-war editorials in their columns. Boards of trade and chambers of commerce added their pleas for the maintenance of peace to those of the business newspapers and magazines. So marked, indeed, was the anti-war solidarity of the financial interests and their spokesmen that the jingoes fell to charging Wall Street with want of patriotism. Wall Street, declared the Sacramento *Evening Bee* (March 11, 1898), was "the colossal and aggregate Benedict Arnold of the Union, and the syndicated Judas Iscariot of humanity." Senator Thurston, of Nebraska, charged that opposition to war was found only among the "money-changers," bringing from the editor of *The American Banker* the reply that "there is not an intelligent, self-respecting and civilized American citizen anywhere who would not prefer to have the existing crisis culminate in peaceful negotiations."

This anti-war attitude on the part of several leading financial journals continued up to the very beginning of hostilities. . . .

The *Commercial and Financial Chronicle* expressed the belief on March 12 that the opposition of the financial interests would yet prevent war; and on April 2 the same journal branded as "monstrous" the proposition to settle the Cuban and "Maine" questions by war while the slightest chance remained for a peaceful solution. On April 16, after the House of Representatives had passed the Cuban resolutions, the Boston *Journal of Commerce* declared: "Sober second thought had but little to do with the deliberations. . . . The members were carried off their feet by the war fever that had been so persistently worked up since the Maine explosion. . . ."

The reasons for this attitude on the part of business are not far to seek. Since the panic of 1893 American business had been in the doldrums. Tendencies toward industrial revival had been checked, first by the Venezuela war scare in December, 1895, and again by the free silver menace in 1896. But in 1897 began a real revival, and before the end of the year signs of prosperity appeared on all sides. The New York *Commercial* conducted a survey of business conditions in a wide variety of trades and industries, from which it concluded that, "after three years of waiting and of false starts, the groundswell of demand has at last begun to rise with a steadiness which leaves little doubt that an era of prosperity has appeared." January, 1898, said the same article, is "a supreme moment in the period of transition from depression to comparative prosperity." This note of optimism one meets at every turn, even in such a careful and conservative sheet as the *Commercial and Financial Chronicle*. As early as July, 1897, this paper remarked: "We appear to be on the eve of a revival in business"; and in December after remarking upon the healthy condition of the railroads and the iron industry, it concluded: "In brief, no one can study the industrial conditions of today in America without a feeling of elation. . . ." The *Wall Street Journal* found only two "blue spots" in the entire country: Boston, which suffered from the depressed demand for cotton goods, and New York, where senseless rate cutting by certain railroads caused uneasiness. "Throughout the west, southwest and on the Pacific coast business has never been better, nor the people more hopeful."

A potent cause for optimism was found in the striking expansion of the American export trade. A volume of exports far in excess of those of any recent year, a favorable balance of trade of $286,000,000, and an especially notable increase in exports of manufactures of iron, steel, and copper, convinced practically every business expert that the United States was on the point of capturing the markets of the world. "There is no question," said one journal, "that the world, generally, is looking more and more to the United States as the source of its supply for very many of the staple commodities of life." Especially elated were spokesmen of the iron and steel industry. Cheaper materials and improved methods were enabling the American producer to undersell his British competitor in Europe and in the British possessions, and Andrew Carnegie was talking of a great shipbuilding yard near New York to take advantage of these low costs. The *Iron Age*, in an editorial on "The Future of Business," foretold the abolition of the business cycle by means of a better planned economy, consolidation of railroads and industries, reduction of margins of profit, higher wages, and lower prices to consumers.

To this fair prospect of a great business revival the threat of war was like a spectre at the feast. A foreign complication, thought the *Commerical and Financial Chronicle* in October, 1897, would quickly mar "the trade prosperity which all are enjoying."

Six months later (April 2, 1898), after a discussion of the effect of war rumors on the stock exchange, it declared: ". . . Every influence has been, and even now is, tending strongly towards a term of decided prosperity, and that the Cuban disturbance, and it alone, has arrested the movement and checked enterprise." The *Banker and Tradesman* saw in the Cuban complication the threat of a "material setback to the prosperous conditions which had just set in after five years of panic and depression." The same journal summarized a calculation made by the Boston *Transcript* showing that in February, 1898, the wave of prosperity had carried the average price of twenty-five leading stocks within 5 ½ points of the high for the preceding ten years and 30 points above the low of 1896, and that the Cuban trouble had, in a little over two months, caused a loss of over ten points, or more than one-third of the recent gain. "War would impede the march of prosperity and put the country back many years," said the *New Jersey Trade Review*. The *Railway Age* was of the opinion that the country was coming out of a depression and needed peace to complete its recovery. "From a commercial and mercenary standpoint," it remarked, "it seems peculiarly bitter that this war should have come when the country had already suffered so much and so needed rest and peace."

The idea that war could bring any substantial benefits to business was generally scouted. It would endanger our currency stability, interrupt our trade, and threaten our coasts and our commerce, thought the *Commercial and Financial Chronicle*. It would "incalculably increase the loss to business interests," said the *Banker's Magazine;* while the *United States Investor* held that war was "never beneficial from a material standpoint, that is, in the long run." The *Railroad Gazette* predicted that war would result in "interruption of business enterprise of every kind, stopping new projects and diminution of the output of existing businesses and contraction of trade everywhere." Railroads would lose more than they would gain. Even arms manufacturers were not all agreed that war would be desirable. Journals speaking for the iron and steel industry also argued that war would injure business. It "would injure the iron and steel makers ten times as much as they would be benefited by the prevailing spurt in the manufacture of small arms, projectiles and steel plates for war ships," in the opinion of one of these. The *American Wool and Cotton Reporter* of New York and the *Northwestern Miller* of Minneapolis agreed that war was never materially beneficial in the long run, while trade journals in Atlanta, Chattanooga, and Portland, Oregon, saw as fruits of the approaching conflict only destruction, debt, and depressed industry.

Many conservative interests feared war for the specific reason that it might derange the currency and even revive the free-silver agitation, which had seemed happily dead. The subsidence of that agitation and the prospect of currency reform were among the hopeful factors at the close of 1897. It was not uncommonly charged that the jingoes were animated in part by the expectation that war would lead to inflation in paper or silver. . . .

Something of a freak among New York financial journals was the *Financial Record*, which, in November, 1897, denounced "the cowardice of our Administration in refusing the phenomenally brave Cubans the commonest rights of belligerency" as "a disgrace to the United States," and argued that war with Spain, far from depressing securities or injuring business, "would vastly increase the net earning power of every security sold on our market today." The mystery of this jingo attitude is explained when we discover that

this journal had been a warm advocate of the free coinage of silver.

Business opinion in the West, especially in the Mississippi Valley, appears to have been less opposed to war and less apprehensive of its results than that of the Atlantic coast. The Kansas City Board of Trade, at the beginning of 1897, had urged recognition of Cuban independence. The Cincinnati Chamber of Commerce, at a meeting on March 29, 1898, adopted "amidst much enthusiasm" resolutions condemning Spain for cruelties to the Cubans and the destruction of the "Maine" and calling for a "firm and vigorous policy which will have for its purpose—peacefully if we can, but with force if we must—the redress of past wrongs, and the complete and unqualified independence of Cuba."

Even in New York, business men saw some rays of light piercing the war clouds. Stock Market operators, according to the *Wall Street Journal*, just after the "Maine" explosion, "did not look for any great break in the market, because actual war with Spain would be a very small affair compared with the Venezuela complication with Great Britain." Their expectation was for a drop in stocks at the beginning of hostilities, followed by a resumption of the recent advance. In fact, the first shock might well be followed by a boom. "The nation looks for peace," declared *Dun's Review*, March 5, "but knows that its sources of prosperity are quite beyond the reach of any attack that is possible." *Bradstreet's* contrasted the jumpiness of Wall Street over war news with "the calm way in which general business interests have regarded the current foreign complications," and *Dun's Review* of March 12 stated that no industry or branch of business showed any restriction, while some had been rapidly gaining, that railroads were increasing their profits while speculators sold their stocks and that there was a growing demand for the products of all the great industries.

Despite such expressions as these, there seems little reason to question the belief that an overwhelming preponderance of the vocal business interests of the country strongly desired peace. By the middle of March, however, many organs of business opinion were admitting that a war with Spain might bring no serious disaster, and there was a growing conviction that such a war was inevitable. In the Senate on March 17, Senator Redfield Proctor, of Vermont, described, from his own observation, the terrible sufferings of the Cuban "reconcentrados." Proctor was supposedly no sensationalist, and his speech carried great weight. The *Wall Street Journal* described its effect among the denizens of the Street. "Senator Proctor's speech," it said, "converted a great many people in Wall Street, who have heretofore taken the ground that the United States had no business to interfere in a revolution on Spanish soil. These men had been among the most prominent in deploring the whole Cuban matter, but there was no question about the accuracy of Senator Proctor's statements and as many of them expressed, they made the blood boil." The *American Banker*, hitherto a firm opponent of intervention, remarked on March 23 that Proctor's speech showed an intolerable state of things, in view of which it could not understand "how any one with a grain of human sympathy within him can dispute the propriety of a policy of intervention, so only that this outraged people might be set free!" It still hoped, however, for a peaceful solution, declaring that the United States ought to urge the Cubans to accept the Spanish offer of autonomy. That this growing conviction that something must be done about Cuba was by no means equivalent to a desire for war, was clearly revealed a few days later. Rumors circulated

to the effect that Spain was willing to sell Cuba and that J. P. Morgan's return from a trip abroad was connected with plans to finance the purchase. "There is much satisfaction expressed in Wall Street," said the *Wall Street Journal*, "at the prospects of having Cuba free, because it is believed that this will take one of the most disturbing factors out of the situation. . . . Even if $200,000,000 is the indemnity demanded it is a sum which the United States could well afford to pay to get rid of the trouble." Even $250,000,000, it was thought, would be insignificant in comparison with the probable cost of war.

It remains to examine the attitude of certain American business men and corporations having an immediate stake in Cuba, or otherwise liable to be directly affected by American intervention. Much American capital, as is well known, was invested in the Cuban sugar industry. Upon this industry the civil war fell with peculiarly devastating effect, not only cutting off profits on capital so invested, but also crippling a valuable carrying trade between Cuba and the United States. Naturally enough, some firms suffering under these conditions desired to see the United States intervene to end the war, though such intervention might lead to war between the United States and Spain. In May, 1897, a memorial on the subject bearing over three hundred signatures was presented to John Sherman, Secretary of State. The signers described themselves as "citizens of the United States, doing business as bankers, merchants, manufacturers, steamship owners and agents in the cities of Boston, New York, Philadelphia, Baltimore, Savannah, Charleston, Jacksonville, New Orleans, and other places, and also other citizens of the United States, who have been for many years engaged in the export and import trade with the Island of Cuba." They called attention to the serious losses to which their businesses had been subjected by the hostilities in Cuba and expressed the hope that, in order to prevent further loss, to reestablish American commerce, and also to secure "the blessings of peace for one and a half millions of residents of the Island of Cuba now enduring unspeakable distress and suffering," the United States Government might take steps to bring about an honorable reconciliation between the parties to the conflict.

Another memorial, signed by many of the same subscribers, was presented to President McKinley on February 9, 1898, by a committee of New York business men. It asserted that the Cuban war, which had now continued for three entire years, had caused an average loss of $100,000,000 a year, or a total loss of $300,000,000 in the import and export trade between Cuba and the United States, to which were to be added "heavy sums irretrievably lost by the destruction of American properties, or properties supported by American capital in the Island itself, such as sugar factories, railways, tobacco plantations, mines and other industrial enterprises; the loss of the United States in trade and capital by means of this war being probably far greater and more serious than that of all the other parties concerned, not excepting Spain herself."

The sugar crop of 1897-1898, continued the memorial, appeared for the most part lost like its two predecessors, and unless peace could be established before May or June of the current year, the crop of 1898-1899, with all the business dependent upon it, would likewise be lost, since the rainy season of summer and fall would be required "to prepare for next winter's crop, by repairing damaged fields, machinery, lines of railways, &c." In view of the importance to the United States of the Cuban trade and of American participation "in the ownership or management of Cuban sugar factories, railways and other enterprises," the petitioners hoped that the President would deem the situation "of sufficient importance as to warrant prompt and efficient measures by our Government, with the sole object of restoring peace . . . and with it restoring to us a most valuable commercial field."

How much weight such pressure from special interests had with the administration there is no way of knowing. But it is to be noted that the pressure from parties directly interested was not all on one side. Mr. E. F. Atkins, an American citizen who divided his time between Boston and his sugar plantation of Soledad near Cienfuegos, Cuba, which he had developed at a cost of $1,400,000, had been able, through protection received from the Spanish Government and through a corps of guards organized and paid by himself, to continue operations throughout the period of the insurrection. He was frequently in Washington, where he had influential friends, during both the Cleveland and McKinley administrations and worked consistently against the adoption of any measures likely to provoke war.

Unlike some of the sugar plantations, American-owned iron mines in Cuba continued to do active business despite the insurrection. Three American iron and manganese enterprises in the single province of Santiago claimed to have an investment of some $6,000,000 of purely American capital, a large proportion of which was in property which could easily be destroyed. "We are fully advised as to our status in case of war," wrote the representative of one company to the Assistant Secretary of State, "and that this property might be subject to confiscation or destruction by the Spanish Government." War between Spain and the United States, wrote the president of another company, "will very likely mean the destruction of our valuable plant and in any event untold loss to our Company and its American stockholders." An American cork company with large interests in Spain; a New York merchant with trade in the Mediterranean and Black Sea; a Mobile firm which had chartered a Spanish ship to carry a cargo of timber—these are samples of American business interests which saw in war the threat of direct damage to themselves. They are hardly offset by the high hopes of an enterprising gentleman of Norfolk, "representing a party of capitalists who are enthusiastic supporters of the Government," who applied to the State Department for a letter of marque "to enable us to lawfully capture Spanish merchant vessels and torpedo boats," adding: "We have secured option on a fine steam vessel and on receipt of proper documents will put to sea forth with."

It seems safe to conclude, from the evidence available, that the only important business interests (other than the business of sensational journalism) which clamored for intervention in Cuba were those directly or indirectly concerned in the Cuban sugar industry; that opposed to intervention were the influence of other parties (including at least one prominent sugar planter) whose business would suffer direct injury from war and also the overwhelming preponderance of general business opinion. After the middle of March, 1898, some conservative editors came to think intervention inevitable on humanitarian grounds, but many of the most influential business journals opposed it to the end.

We can now turn to the question whether American business was imperialistic; whether, in other words, business opinion favored schemes for acquiring foreign territory to supply it with markets, fields for capital investment, or commercial and naval stations in distant parts of the world. American business men were not unaware of the struggle for colonies then raging among European nations. Did they feel that the United States ought to participate in that struggle?

We have seen above that the rising tide of prosperity was intimately connected with the increase in American exports, particularly of manufactured articles. That the future welfare of American industry was dependent upon the command of foreign markets was an opinion so common as to appear almost universal. The New York *Journal of Commerce* pointed out, early in 1897, that the nation's industrial plant had been developed far beyond the needs of domestic consumption. In the wire nail industry there was said to be machinery to make four times as many nails as the American markets could consume. Rail mills, locomotive shops, and glass factories were in a similar situation. "Nature has thus destined this country for the industrial supremacy of the world," said the same paper later in the year. When the National Association of Manufacturers met in New York for its annual convention in January, 1898, "the discussion of ways and means for extending this country's trade, and more particularly its export business, was, in fact, almost the single theme of the speakers," according to *Bradstreet's,* which added the comment: "Nothing is more significant of the changed attitude toward this country's foreign trade manifested by the American manufacturer today as compared with a few years ago, than the almost single devotion which he pays to the subject of possible export-trade extension."

But if business men believed, prior to the opening of the war with Spain, that foreign markets were to be secured through the acquisition of colonies, they were strangely silent about it. To the program of colonial expansion which for almost a decade had been urged by such men as Mahan, Albert Shaw, Lodge, Roosevelt, and Morgan, business had remained, to all appearances, either indifferent or antagonistic. To the business man, such a program was merely one form of dangerous jingoism. A large section of business opinion had, indeed, favored plans for the building of a Nicaraguan canal with governmental assistance, and some spokesmen for business had favored annexation of the Hawaiian Islands. But beyond these relatively modest projects few business men, apparently, wished to go. Two of the most important commercial journals, the New York *Journal of Commerce* and the *Commercial and Financial Chronicle*, had stoutly opposed both the canal scheme and Hawaiian annexation. The former satirized the arguments of the proponents of both schemes. "We must certainly build the canal to defend the islands, and it is quite clear that we must acquire the islands . . . in order to defend the canal." The canal was not only unnecessary, but unless fortified at each end and patrolled by two fleets, it would be a positive misfortune. Such protection—"the price of jingoism"—might "easily cost us $25,000,000 a year, besides the lump sum that will be required for the original investment, and there is absolutely no excuse whatever in our commercial or our political interests for a single step in this long procession of expenses and of complications with foreign powers." As for Hawaii and Cuba, neither was fit for self-government as a state—and the American constitution provided no machinery for governing dependencies. The Hawaiian Islands would have no military value unless the United States were to build a great navy and take an aggressive attitude in the Pacific. The *Commerical and Financial Chronicle* saw in colonies only useless outposts which

must be protected at great expense, and the St. Louis *Age of Steel* warned lest the expansion of the export trade might "lead to territorial greed, as in the case of older nations, the price of which in armaments and militarism offsets the gain made by the spindle and the forge."

Colonies were not only certain to bear a fruit of danger and expense; they were valueless from the commercial point of view. Did not the colonies of Great Britain afford us one of the most valuable of our export markets? Did we not trade as advantageously with Guiana, a British colony, as with independent Venezuela? "Most of our ideas of the commercial value of conquests, the commercial uses of navies and the commercial advantages of political control," said the New York *Journal of Commerce*, dated back to times when colonial policies were designed to monopolize colonial trade for the mother country. The *Commercial and Financial Chronicle* believed that the current European enthusiasm for colonies was based on false premises; for although trade often followed the flag, "the trade is not always with the home markets of the colonizer. England and the United States are quite as apt to slip in with their wares under the very Custom-House pennant of the French or German dependency." Outright opposition, such as this, to the idea of colonial expansion is not common in the business periodicals examined; much more common is complete silence on the subject. Positive and negative evidence together seem to warrant the conclusion that American business in general, at the opening of 1898, was either indifferent to imperialism, or definitely opposed.

By suggesting that McKinley and certain American business men had a clearly defined Cuban policy, WALTER LaFEBER has addressed his work to many of the assumptions, implications, and conclusions of Julius W. Pratt's *Expansionists of 1898*. In the process, LaFeber has helped to provide a reinterpretation of the origins of the Spanish-American War. Specifically, LaFeber plays down the role of yellow journalists and various expansionist groups as forces that led the country to war, while he attributes responsibility to McKinley and various segments of the business community. But has LaFeber actually demonstrated that the business community influenced McKinley's policies?°

McKinley, the Business Community, and Cuba

Elections in 1897 had not gone well for McKinley's party, nor had more recent elections in New York and Kentucky. During the first three months of 1898 the President and other Republican leaders received many letters which drew bleak pictures of the party's future if the administration failed to deal with Cuba immediately. McKinley's letters on this point were capped with a long message from Henry Cabot Lodge on March 21. Lodge had recently returned from taking a private poll of Massachusetts opinion. The Senator first assured McKinley that the masses were firmly behind the administration. But, Lodge continued, "if the war in Cuba drags on through the summer with nothing done

we should go down in the greatest defeat ever known before the cry 'Why have you not settled the Cuban question.'" Clarence Cary, who opposed a strong Cuban policy, wrote in the *Journal of Commerce* in late March that mail was pouring in "even from conservative city districts" warning of the Republican losses which would inevitably result if the Democrats could "proclaim from every stump that it was they who forced the hand of the Republican President and with the aid of a few Republicans secured the liberty of Cuba." These letters, Cary concluded, were having a "potent effect."

Most of the "conservative city districts" which Cary mentioned had long opposed

---

war with Spain. There were exceptions, however. The American business community was by no means monolithic in its opposition to war. To say as a generalization that businessmen opposed war is as erroneous as saying that businessmen wanted war. It is possible to suggest, however, that by the middle of March important businessmen and spokesmen for the business community were advocating war. It is also possible to suggest that at the same time, a shift seemed to be occurring in the general business community regarding its over-all views on the desirability of war.

Financial journals which advocated bimetallism had long urged a stronger attitude toward Spain in the hope that the resulting conflict would force the Treasury to pay expenses in silver. More important, business spokesmen in such midwestern and western cities as Cincinnati, Louisville, St. Louis, Chicago, San Francisco, and especially Pittsburgh were not reluctant to admit that they would welcome war. . . .

A strong possibility exists that the antiwar commercial journals in New York spoke for the less important members of that financial community. Russell Sage, claiming that he spoke "not only my own views on this point, but those of other moneyed men with whom I have talked," demanded that if the "Maine" was blown up by an outside force "the time for action has come. There should be no wavering." If war did occur, "There is no question as to where the rich men stand"; they would buy government bonds as they had during the Civil War and do all in their power to bolster the nation's war resources. W. C. Beer, who attempted to make a thorough survey of leading businessmen's opinion, concluded that "the steady opponents of the war among financiers were simply the life insurance men and small bankers." Beer found such giants as John Jacob Astor, John Gates, Thomas Fortune Ryan,

William Rockefeller, and Stuyvesant Fish "feeling militant." On March 28 J.Pierpont Morgan declared that further talk of arbitration would accomplish nothing.

Beer's findings can be supplemented with an analysis of the membership of the Cuban League of the United States. This organization began advertising in early 1897 that it would gladly receive donations to finance its efforts to free Cuba from Spanish control. As a part of these efforts, the league sold bonds for the Cuban Junta. This organization included such militants as Theodore Roosevelt, Colonel Ethan Allen, and Charles A. Dana. But the following conservative businessmen were among the Vice-Presidents: J. Edward Simmons, former President of the New York Stock Exchange, President of the Fourth National Bank of New York; Thomas F. Gilroy, builder and real estate operator in New York City; Chauncey M. Depew, railroad president and director of numerous railway and banking corporations; Thomas L. James, Chairman of the Board of Lincoln National Bank in New York City, President of the Lincoln Safe Deposit Company; John R. Dos Passos, New York lawyer who engaged in banking, corporate, and financial law and who had been active in the formation of large business amalgamations, including the sugar trust. Seated on the Board of Directors were General Daniel Butterfield, Civil War hero, bank president, and Executive Officer of the Steam Boat and Ferry Company; and Colonel John Jacob Astor.

A group of interests that depended upon Cuban trade formed another category of business support which demanded that the revolution be terminated. A group of importers, exporters, bankers, manufacturers, and steamship and vessel owners sent McKinley a petition in February, 1898, which noted that the fighting had created a loss of one hundred million dollars a year in business conducted directly with the island, not to mention the destruction of American properties on the island. The petition demanded peace before the rainy season in May; otherwise, the sugar crop of 1898 and 1899 would be ruined. Those who signed this petition included "a large number of well-known and influential firms" in New York City, the New York *Tribune* noted, and also the names of businessmen in Philadelphia and Mobile.

The petition noted the immense losses suffered by property owners and merchants who had invested in the island itself. By early 1898 these persons were becoming alarmed about something other than the day-to-day destruction of property, although this was certainly troublesome. The State Department began receiving reports that, as Fitzhugh Lee phrased the problem, "there may be a revolution within a revolution." Conservative interests feared that continued Spanish rule or autonomy, no matter how developed, would result in Cuban radical forces gaining control of the government. A strong feeling was growing which demanded American intervention to end this threat. The American Consul in Santiago summarized this feeling on March 23, 1898: "Property holders without distinction of nationality, and with but few exceptions, strongly desire annexation, having but little hope of a stable government under either of the contending forces. . . .[B]ut such a move would not be popular among the masses." These interests, the Consul reported, regretted that Americans did not favor outright, immediate annexation. McKinley learned of this sentiment from a letter written by "a gentleman of high standing, who has close personal relations with influential Cubans who have favored the rebellion," as Levi P. Morton, former Vice-President under Harrison and a wheel-horse of the Republican party, described the author. This letter

warned that the rebellion had to end quickly or the radical classes would come to power. The writer believed that educated and wealthy backers of the rebellion now wanted either annexation or autonomy under American control. "They are most pronounced in their fears," he continued, "that independence, if obtained, would result in the troublesome, adventurous and nonresponsible class" seizing power.

Many of these businessmen in Cuba hoped that annexation could be accomplished through peaceful means, but they found themselves trapped when they realized that Spain would not surrender her sovereignty on American terms without war. Among those who were so trapped was Edwin F. Atkins, one of the largest American investors in Cuban plantations. He deprecated the possibility of war on behalf of the insurgents, especially since the protection provided by Spanish troops enabled his plantations to continue their harvests throughout the revolution. But as early as January, 1897, Atkins had written Lodge that the best thing that could happen would be the annexation of Cuba by the United States. . . .

Perhaps the American business community exerted the most influence on the administration during the last two weeks in March when influential business spokesmen began to welcome the possibility of war in order to end the suspense which shrouded the commercial exchanges. Although other historians have touched briefly on this important change, it should be noted that some important business spokesmen and President McKinley apparently arrived at this decision at approximately the same time.

During the first two months of 1898 the United States began to enjoy prosperous conditions for the first time in five years. The de Lôme and "Maine" incidents affected business conditions only in the stock exchanges, and even there the impact was slight. Business improved, especially in the West and Northwest. In early March very few business journals feared a return of depression conditions, and with the gold influx resulting from discoveries in Alaska and from the export surplus, even fewer business observers displayed anxiety over the silver threat.

But in mid-March financial reporters noted that business in commodities as well as stocks had suddenly slowed. Henry Clay Frick had been optimistic in his business reports to Andrew Carnegie, who was vacationing in Scotland. But on March 24, Frick reported that "owing to uncertainty. . .of the Cuban trouble, business is rather stagnant." A Wall Street correspondent wrote on March 22 that "the last two days have been the dullest for many a month." On March 26 the *Commercial and Financial Chronicle* summarized the situation. No "sudden and violent drop in prices" had occurred. But the rapid progress in trade had stopped and now "frequent complaints are heard. The volume of trade undoubtedly remains large, but the reports speak of new enterprises being held in check."

Businessmen had been particularly influenced by the speech of Senator Redfield Proctor of Vermont on March 17. Proctor was known for his conservative, antiwar disposition, an attitude he shared with his intimate friend, William McKinley. But the Senator had just returned from a visit to Cuba, a visit that had profoundly shocked him. Proctor discounted Spanish reforms as "too late," but he advised against going to war over the "Maine." The United States should use force, Proctor intimated, only to deliver the Cuban people from "the worst misgovernment of which I ever had knowledge." Conversations with businessmen in Cuba had provided him with most of his information; these men had declared "without exception" that it was too late for

any more schemes of autonomy. They wanted an American protectorate, annexation, or a free Cuba. Although Proctor did not say so explicitly, none of these solutions was immediately possible without war with Spain. This speech deeply impressed almost all of the conservative and business journals which had opposed war. Many of these journals did not overlook Proctor's role as one of McKinley's "most trusted advisors and friends." Two weeks later the New York *Commercial Advertiser* looked back and marked this speech as the turning point in the road to war. . . .

Perhaps the most influential note the President received that week was a telegram from W. C. Reick, a trusted political adviser in New York City and city editor of the New York *Herald*. This message arrived at the White House on March 25: "Big corporations here now believe we will have war. Believe all would welcome it as relief to suspense." On March 27, the New York *Tribune* ran a front-page article which indicated that Reick's evaluation also applied to the London Stock Exchange, a financial institution which some American investors considered of more importance than the New York Exchange. "What is wanted first of all is relief from the suspense. . . . Even a declaration of war would be preferred by bankers and stockbrokers to the continuance of a stagnant market, with hourly flurries, caused by sensational journalism and the rumors of impending hostilities," the *Tribune* reported. If war occurred, a "speculators' movement" might result in a "temporary flurry in American stocks." But other investors would hold their securities "in confident expectation that these will rise with the increased movement of railway traffic caused by war."

Two days after the receipt of Reick's telegram, McKinley and Day presented an ultimatum to Spain. This move climaxed a week of hurried consultations and policy changes. Before March 20 the President had considered purchasing the island or attempting to work out a plan which would ensure American control while maintaining the trappings of Spanish sovereignty. Spain refused to sell the island, however, and the Junta and the rebels on the island would not listen to the second proposal. Now in the new climate created by Proctor's speech and the changing ideas of the business community, McKinley prepared to take more forceful steps. For the first time in the crisis the President called in a number of Democratic senators for consultations on March 22. Doubtlessly reflecting the changed attitudes of both McKinley and some business spokesmen, the war party in the Senate now claimed for the first time a majority of the forty-three Republicans, including representatives of the large corporations. These changes threatened to provoke Congress into its most belligerent outbursts on March 29 and 30. . . .

McKinley had had the choice of three policies which would have terminated the Cuban revolution. First, he could have left the Spanish forces and the insurgents fight until one or the other fell exhausted from the bloodshed and financial strain. During the struggle the United States could have administered food and medicine to the civilian population, a privilege which the Spanish agreed to allow in March, 1898. Second, the President could have demanded an armistice and Spanish assurances that negotiations over the summer would result in some solution which would pacify American feelings. That is to say, he could have followed Woodford's ideas. Third, McKinley could have demanded both an armistice and Spanish assurances that Cuba would become independent immediately. If Spain would not grant both of these conditions, American military intervention would result. The last was the course the President followed.

Each of these policy alternatives deserves a short analysis. For American policy makers, the first choice was the least acceptable of the three, but the United States did have to deal, nevertheless, with certain aspects of this policy. If Spain hoped to win such a conflict, she had to use both the carrot of an improved and attractive autonomy scheme and the stick of an increased and effective military force. Spain could have granted no amount of autonomy, short of complete independence, which would have satisfied the rebels, and whether Americans cared to admit it or not, they were at least partially responsible for this obstinacy on the part of the insurgents. The United States did attempt to stop filibustering expeditions, but a large number nevertheless reached Cuban shores. More important, when the Spanish Minister asked Day to disband the New York Junta, the financial taproot of the insurgent organization, the Assistant Secretary replied that "this was not possible under American law and in the present state of public feeling." Woodford had given the Spanish Queen the same reply in mid-January. It was perhaps at this point that Spain saw the last hopes for a negotiated peace begin to flicker away.

Seemingly unrelated actions by the United States gave boosts to the rebel cause. The sending of the "Maine," for instance, considerably heartened the rebels; they believed that the warship diverted Spanish attention and military power from insurgent forces. When the vessel exploded, the New York Junta released a statement which did not mourn the dead sailors as much as it mourned the sudden disappearance of American power in Havana harbor. The Junta interpreted the passage of the $50,000,000 war appropriation measure during the first week of March as meaning either immediate war or the preparation for war. Under such conditions, it was not odd that the rebels were reluctant to compromise their objective of complete independence.

If the insurgents would not have accepted autonomy, no matter how liberal or attractive, then Spain might have hoped to suppress the rebels with outright force. To have done so, however, the Spanish government would have had to bring its army through the rainy season with few impairments, resume to a large extent the *reconcentrado* policies, and prevent all United States aid from reaching the rebels. The first objective would have been difficult, but the last two, if carried out, would have meant war with the United States. The State Department could not allow Spain to reimpose methods even faintly resembling Weyler's techniques, nor could the Department have allowed the searching of American vessels. McKinley and the American people hoped that Spain would stop the revolution, but they also insisted on taking from Spain the only tools with which that nation could deal with the Cubans.

Having found this first alternative impossible to accept, McKinley might have chosen a second approach: demand an armistice and ultimate pacification of the island, but attempt to achieve this peacefully over several months and with due respect for the sovereignty of Spain. This was the alternative Woodford hoped the administration would choose. He had reported during the two weeks before McKinley's message that the Spanish had given in time and time again on points which he had believed they could not afford to grant. In spite of the threat of revolution from the army, the Queen had granted a temporary truce. The American Minister continued to ask for more time to find a peaceful settlement. On April 11, the day the war message went to Congress, Woodford wrote the President, "To-day it is just possible that Moret and I have been

right [in our pursuit of peace], but it is too soon to be jubilant." The American Minister sincerely believed that the negotiations during the period of truce could, with good faith on both the American and Spanish sides, result in Spain evacuating the island. This would have to be done slowly, however. No sovereign nation could be threatened with a time limit and uncompromising demands without fighting back. The fact that Spain would not grant McKinley's demand for immediate Cuban independence makes the Spanish-American War which began in April, 1898, by no means an inevitable conflict. Any conflict is inevitable once one proud and sovereign power, dealing with a similar power, decides to abandon the conference table and issue an ultimatum. The historical problem remains: which power took the initiative in setting the conditions that resulted in armed conflict, and were those conditions justified?

By April 10 McKinley had assumed an inflexible position. The President abjured this second alternative and demanded not only a truce, but a truce which would lead to a guarantee of immediate Cuban independence obtained with the aid of American mediation. He moreover demanded such a guarantee of independence before the Cortes or the Cuban parliament, the two groups which had the constitutional power to grant such independence, were to gather for their formal sessions.

The central question is, of course, why McKinley found himself in such a position on April 10 that only the third alternative was open to him. The President did not want war; he had been sincere and tireless in his efforts to maintain the peace. By mid-March, however, he was beginning to discover that, although he did not want war, he did want what only a war could provide: the disappearance of the terrible uncertainty in American political and economic life, and a solid basis from which to resume the building of the new American commercial empire. When the President made his demands, therefore, he made the ultimate demands; as far as he was concerned, a six-month period of negotiations would not serve to temper the political and economic problems in the United States, but only exacerbate them.

To say this is to raise another question: why did McKinley arrive at this position during mid-March? What were the factors which limited the President's freedom of choice and policies at this particular time? The standard interpretations of the war's causes emphasize the yellow journals and a belligerent Congress. These were doubtlessly crucial factors in shaping the course of American entry into the conflict, but they must be used carefully. A first observation should be that Congress and the yellow press, which had been loudly urging intervention ever since 1895, did not make a maiden appearance in March, 1898; new elements had to enter the scene at that time to act as the catalysts for McKinley's policy. Other facts should be noted regarding the yellow press specifically. In areas where this press supposedly was most important, such as New York City, no more than one-third of the press could be considered sensational. The strongest and most widespread prowar journalism apparently occurred in the Midwest. But there were few yellow journals there. The papers that advocated war in this section did so for reasons other than sensationalism; among these reasons were the influence of the Cuban Junta and, perhaps most important, the belief that the United States possessed important interests in the Caribbean area which had to be protected. Finally, the yellow press obviously did not control the levers of American foreign policy. McKinley held these, and he bitterly attacked the owners of the sensational

journals as "evil disposed...people." An interpretation stressing rabid journalism as a major cause of the war should draw some link to illustrate how these journals reached the White House or the State Department. To say that this influence was exerted through public opinion proves nothing; the next problem is to demonstrate how much public opinion was governed by the yellow press, how much of this opinion was influenced by more sober factors, and which of these two branches of opinion most influenced McKinley.

Congress was a hotbed of interventionist sentiment, but then it had been so since 1895. The fact was that Congress had more trouble handling McKinley than the President had handling Congress. The President had no fear of that body. He told Charles Dawes during the critical days of February and March that if Congress tried to adjourn he would call it back into session. McKinley held Congress under control until the last two days of March, when the publication of the "Maine" investigation forced Thomas B. Reed, the passionately antiwar Speaker of the House, to surrender to the onslaughts of the rapidly increasing interventionist forces. . . .

When the Senate threatened to overrule the President's orders that the declaration of war not include a recognition of Cuban independence, the White House whipped its supporters into line and forced the Senate to recede from its position. This was an all-out battle between the White House and a strong Senate faction. McKinley triumphed despite extremely strong pressure exerted by sincere American sentiment on behalf of immediate Cuban independence and despite the more crass material interests of the Junta's financial supporters and spokesmen. The President wanted to have a free hand in dealing with Cuba after the war, and Congress granted his wishes. Events on Capitol Hill may have been more colorful than those at the White House, but the latter, nor the former, was the center of power in March and April, 1898.

Influences other than the yellow press or congressional belligerence were more important in shaping McKinley's position of April 11. Perhaps most important was the transformation of the opinion of many spokesmen for the business community who had formerly opposed war. If, as one journal declared, the McKinley administration, "more than any that have preceded it, sustains. . .close relations to the business interests of the country," then this change of business sentiment should not be discounted. This transformation brought important financial spokesmen, especially from the Northeast, into much the same position that had long been occupied by prointerventionist business groups and journals in the trans-Appalachian area. McKinley's decision to intervene placated many of the same business spokesmen whom he had satisfied throughout 1897 and January and February of 1898 by his refusal to declare war.

Five factors may be delineated which shaped this interventionist sentiment of the business community. First, some business journals emphasized the material advantages to be gained should Cuba become a part of the world in which the United States would enjoy, in the words of the New York *Commercial Advertiser*, "full freedom of development in the whole world's interest." The *Banker's Magazine* noted that "so many of our citizens are so involved in the commerce and productions of the island, that to protect these interests. . .the United States will have eventually to force the establishment of fair and reasonable government." The material damage suffered by investors in Cuba and by many merchants, manufacturers, exporters, and importers, as, for example, the groups

which presented the February 10 petition to McKinley, forced these interests to advocate a solution which could be obtained only through force.

A second reason was the uncertainty that plagued the business community in mid-March. This uncertainty was increased by Proctor's powerful and influential speech and by the news that a Spanish torpedo-boat flotilla was sailing from Cadiz to Cuba. The uncertainty was exemplified by the sudden stagnation of trade on the New York Stock Exchange after March 17. Such an unpredictable economic basis could not provide the springboard for the type of overseas commercial empire that McKinley and numerous business spokesmen envisioned.

Third, by March many businessmen who had deprecated war on the ground that the United States Treasury did not possess adequate gold reserves began to realize that they had been arguing from false assumptions. The heavy exports of 1897 and the discoveries of gold in Alaska and Australia brought the yellow metal into the country in an ever widening stream. Private bankers had been preparing for war since 1897. *Banker's Magazine* summarized these developments: "Therefore, while not desiring war, it is apparent that the country now has an ample coin basis for sustaining the credit operations which a conflict would probably make necessary. In such a crisis the gold standard will prove a bulwark of confidence."

Fourth, antiwar sentiment lost much strength when the nation realized that it had nothing to fear from European intervention on the side of Spain. France and Russia, who were most sympathetic to the Spanish monarchy, were forced to devote their attention to the Far East. Neither of these nations wished to alienate the United States on the Cuban issue. More important, Americans happily realized that they had the support of Great Britain. The *rapprochement* which had occurred since the Venezuelan incident now paid dividends. On an official level, the British Foreign Office assured the State Department that nothing would be accomplished in the way of European intervention unless the United States requested such intervention. The British attitude made it easy for McKinley to deal with a joint European note of April 6 which asked for American moderation toward Spain. The President brushed off the request firmly but politely. On an unofficial level, American periodicals expressed appreciation of the British policy on Cuba, and some of the journals noted that a common Anglo-American approach was also desirable in Asia. The European reaction is interesting insofar as it evinces the continental powers' growing realization that the United States was rapidly becoming a major force in the world. But the European governments set no limits on American dealings with Spain. McKinley could take the initiative and make his demands with little concern for European reactions.

Finally, opposition to war melted away in some degree when the administration began to emphasize that the United States enjoyed military power much superior to that of Spain. One possible reason for McKinley's policies during the first two months of 1898 might have been his fear that the nation was not adequately prepared. As late as the weekend of March 25 the President worried over this inadequacy. But in late February and early March, especially after the $50,000,000 appropriation by Congress, the country's military strength developed rapidly. On March 13

the Philadelphia *Press* proclaimed that American naval power greatly exceeded that of the Spanish forces. By early April those who feared a Spanish bombardment of New York City were in the small minority. More representative were the views of Winthrop Chanler who wrote Lodge that if Spanish troops invaded New York "they would all be absorbed in the population. . .and engaged in selling oranges before they got as far as 14th Street."

As the words of McKinley's war message flew across the wires to Madrid, many business spokesmen who had opposed war had recently changed their minds, American military forces were rapidly growing more powerful, banks and the United States Treasury had secured themselves against the initial shocks of war, and the European powers were divided among themselves and preoccupied in the Far East. Business boomed after McKinley signed the declaration of war. "With a hesitation so slight as to amount almost to indifference," *Bradstreet's* reported on April 30, "the business community, relieved from the tension caused by the incubus of doubt and uncertainty which so long controlled it, has stepped confidently forward to accept the situation confronting it owing to the changed conditions." "Unfavorable circumstances. . .have hardly excited remark, while the stimulating effects have been so numerous and important as to surprise all but the most optimistic," this journal concluded. A new type of American empire, temporarily clothed in armor, stepped out on the international stage after a half century of preparation to make its claim as one of the great world powers.

LOUIS J. HALLE (1910-   ), a professor of foreign
affairs at the University of Virginia and a frequent writer
about American foreign policy, has long been concerned
about the impact that mass democracy has had on the
quality of American foreign relations. In regard to the
Spanish-American War, Halle, unlike LaFeber, views
McKinley as a president who was unable to lead the
country in the spring of 1898 and who reluctantly followed
the public clamor for war. Halle is also troubled by the fact
that policy makers must often act under great pressures of
the moment, frequently without time to reflect upon the
consequences of their action. In this respect, he is highly
critical of the McKinley Administration for permitting
military considerations to shape political policies during
the Spanish-American War. Contrary to Halle, other
historians have argued that McKinley was very much
aware of the political consequences of his military
decisions.°

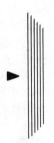

► *Drifting War Policies*

The modern history of American foreign
policy, as distinct from its ancient history,
begins in 1898. Up to 1898 the United
States had cultivated and enjoyed the isolation implicit in the geographical concept
of two hemispheres. In 1898 it lost or gave up
that isolation by assuming commitments
overseas. It entered the arena of European
rivalries as a newly arrived world power. All
this, as we shall see, was implicit in its acquisition of the Phillippine Islands as a
piece of real estate outside the New
World. . . .

This engagement in overseas imperialism was so abrupt and unpremeditated,
however, and we were so little prepared for
it, that our thinking could not adjust itself.
We could not grasp what it meant for our

isolation and, consequently, our isolationism. For almost half a century after our
isolation was gone we still clung to the isolationist policy. Only a nation with such vast
reserves of strength as we had could have
survived this failure of understanding to
keep up with change. As it was, the price we
had to pay was high. We are still paying it
today in many ways, including the present
weakness of our diplomatic and strategic
position in the Far East. But all this will
come out in what follows.

One might say that the nineteenth
century ends in the 1890's with a period of
transition leading to the birth of the twentieth century in 1914. Up through the
1890's the *Pax Britannica* had dominated
the world. Britain held the balance of

°Pages 176-189 *Dream and Reality* by Louis J. Halle. Copyright © 1958, 1959 by Louis J. Halle, Jr.
Reprinted by permission of Harper & Row and George Allen & Unwin Ltd. Footnotes omitted.

power in Europe. She protected the independence of the American hemisphere. And in the competition for empire around the rim of Asia—a competition that represented an extension of the power contests in Europe—she had the chief role.

But a fundamental change took place in the 1890's with the appearance on the world scene of three new powers: Germany, Japan, and the United States. All three were suddenly realizing their potential strength; all three were being tempted by dreams of what that strength might gain for them; all three were unseasoned, like children who have grown up suddenly to possess an adult strength beyond their wisdom and experience.

Both Germany and Japan, in a sort of ecstasy of power, embarked on a course of empire that was to lead to the crashing collisions of the twentieth century. The United States, in the 1890's, briefly felt the same impulse, tentatively embarked on the same course, made commitments that would plague her, and then subsided again under the overriding sway of her liberal and isolationist traditions alike. After her one brief adventure in empire she retired. She emerged from her retirement and her strength became available to check that of Germany and Japan only when disaster was already upon the world. One might say that Germany and Japan used their newly found strength to disrupt world order, while the United States withheld its newly found strength from the maintenance of world order.

Quite aside from the overseas commitment which we Americans acquired in 1898, the ending of the *Pax Britannica* was bound, in itself, to end our putative isolation. When our surrounding oceans were no longer securely dominated by a power that was well disposed to us we would find ourselves vitally dependent on the outcome of political and military contests across those oceans. Our own security would require us to pursue an active diplomacy designed to prevent any hostile or potentially hostile power on the other side from dominating them.

For the moment, however, I am not concerned with this larger picture. I am concerned with what appears to have been a deliberately assumed commitment on the far side of the Pacific, a commitment which could not have been brought into any logical or practical correspondence with the continuation of an isolationism based on independence of Old World politics. This inconsistency would have been obvious if we had acquired Ireland as a colonial possession which we had to defend. Immediately we would have become, unmistakably, a power in the Old World, deep in its politics. In our acquisition of the Philippines this may have been less obvious, but it was no less true. The Philippines were at the heart of a distant area in which the rival European powers and Japan, greedy for empire, deployed substantially more strength than we did. If we were to defend the Philippines, we would have to muster some military strength of our own in the area and we would have to enter upon the diplomatic game of playing the other powers off against one another. Because we did not see this, the historical record reveals a direct line of causation from our acquisition of the Philippine commitment in 1898 to the Japanese attack on Pearl Harbor in 1941, an attack that coincided with the temporary Japanese capture of the Philippines. Perhaps that same line of causation can be traced even to the Korean War and our conflict with Communist China.

Virtually everyone would agree, today, that it was a mistake to acquire the Philippines and, at the same time, seek to continue our isolationist policy. Most students of the subject, I think, would also agree that, whatever our policy, it was still a mistake to acquire the Philippines. Their possession served no strategic interest but was, rather, a strategic liability, especially as, with the passage of time, it came to represent a challenge to Japan. And what we got from the Philippines in markets and trade was far less than what it cost us to administer and defend them. The Philippines would have been useful to us only if, as a handful of American imperialists in 1898 wanted us to do, we had set out to dominate the world. In fact, however, they were pure burden from start to finish, and we had to recognize them as such. But, once the fateful mistake of acquiring them was made, we were stuck with them, and it is clear that even today, when they have at last become independent, their defense is still a charge upon us. In meeting that charge we have added the defense of Japan, Korea, and Formosa to the burden we already bore.

I am interested in the particular question of how we came, in 1898, to make this strategic misstep. And I mean to explore the question. . . not for its own sake but because it seems to me to epitomize the limitations under which statesmen everywhere labor and the compulsion of circumstance that tends to shape the policy of every nation. In other words, such an examination should suggest how history actually is made, and that is its real value.

What I have to say here is the product of an extended investigation of the source materials and the historical interpretations that bear on the question. I started this investigation with the common view that a quite avoidable blunder had been made by the administration of President McKinley in acquiring the Philippines. I wanted to find out at what particular point in the sequence of events the mistake had been made, and by whom, and on the basis of what thinking. I supposed that there was one day and one hour and one place where

one man or a group of men had decided that we should take the Philippines, when he or they were quite free to decide that we should not take them. By the time I finished my investigation, however, I had concluded instead that, given the total situation at the time, it would have been virtually impossible for the McKinley administration to have avoided the acquisition of the Philippines. I never did find the single point in the drift of events where its tendency could have been stopped or turned back, where the administration, consequently, really had a choice in the matter— even when it thought that it did have such a choice and was exercising it. If we understand this, in the particular case under scrutiny, we shall understand much better how foreign policy in general develops and is determined—today no less than in the past.

Having presented my conclusion in advance, let me add that it does not necessarily imply historical predestination. I assume, still, that history is made by men who have a certain freedom of choice. But I am impressed by the heavy compulsions that drive them to make one choice rather than another, so that the freedom they enjoy is to oppose forces that are generally too great for them.

Most of us Americans remember, from our history lessons, the Spanish-American War of 1898. This was the first display of that strength which made us a world power. On this occasion we used that strength, as became our liberal tradition, for the liberation of the long-suffering Cubans from the tyranny of Spain. This we all remember. What few of us remember is the Philippine War, which began two days before the formal conclusion of the Spanish-American War, which lasted some four years, and which was substantially more costly in blood and treasure alike. In this second and much heavier war we Ameri-

cans, to our horror, found ourselves engaged in desperate combat with the distant
Filipinos who were resisting our attempt to
subjugate them. We have good reason for
not wanting to remember this war, in which
we became engaged without any intention
and essentially against our own will. How
was it, then, that we found ourselves
fighting to conquer a land off the shores of
Asia which, as was widely apparent, we
would have done well to refuse as a gift?

When we went to war with Spain on
April 25, 1898, virtually no one in the
United States had any notion of acquiring
an Asiatic empire. It was an exceptional
American who knew where the Philippine
Islands were, or perhaps, had even heard of
them. Those whom we identify today with
their acquisition appear to have had no
thought, as yet, of acquiring them. Apparently it was not in the mind of Theodore
Roosevelt, then Assistant Secretary of the
Navy, when he made the arrangements for
Commodore Dewey's attack on the Spanish
squadron at Manila; it had not occurred to
the Commodore; and Captain Mahan, the
philosopher of expansionism, experienced
misgivings when it first appeared that we
might be committed to their acquisition.

Not only did we have no thought of acquiring the Philippines before we entered
upon the course of action by which they
became ours, their acquisition, if it had
been proposed, would have been regarded
as repugnant to our national policy. We
believed that a nation like ours, dedicated
to representative government with the
consent of the governed, could not include
within its jurisdiction some seven million
distant subjects, unqualified for citizenship, over which it exercised the kind of
colonial rule against which it had declared
its own independence. Many Americans
questioned whether our Constitution, with
its guarantees of human rights, would allow
it. Even if these bars had not existed, our

people had shown before, as they have
shown since, their aversion for the kind of
empire which the European great powers
had been establishing among the "lesser
breeds." Yet the fact remains that, early in
1899, we found ourselves already committed to the prosecution of a long and
painful war for the subjugation of the Philippines. Our virtually unquestioned policy
was one thing; our action was the opposite.
How could this be?

The Spanish-American War was not
made by statesmen acting with delib-
eration, weighing their responsibilities, and
taking the requirements of national policy
as their guide. In 1898 our nation, for the
moment, lost its sobriety and abandoned
itself to glory. This was a people's war into
which our government was swept by public
opinion.

What does it mean to say this? Who were
the people? What was public opinion?

Public opinion, as far as governments are
concerned, is not the spontaneous expression of the population as a statistical
total. It is, rather, the opinion expressed by
those who can influence significant parts of
that population to a degree which might be
politically decisive. In 1898 this meant,
most notably, newspaper publishers. The
yellow press, competing in sensationalism,
deliberately embarked on a campaign
against Spanish treatment of the Cubans as
a means of increasing its circulation. It
elaborated atrocity stories to arouse alike the
animal passion and the self-righteousness
of its readers. For this and other reasons
public pressures were developed, emotional pressures of a nature hard for any
government to deal with; since to those
who do not share their sobriety the reasons
of the sober sound like the counsels of cowardice.

Historians generally recognize today
that we had no legitimate *casus belli*
against Spain. Her inherited position in

Cuba and Puerto Rico, a last remnant of her empire in the New World, had become obsolete and increasingly untenable by the end of the nineteenth century. It would have to be adjusted. But the Spanish government recognized this, and there was no reason to doubt that, given time, patience, and the absence of public excitement in either country, the adjustment could be accomplished without war. It had, in fact, almost been accomplished before the war broke out. The Spanish government, moving as fast as an impassioned public opinion in its own country allowed, was cooperating earnestly with our government to achieve a diplomatic solution. Twenty days before we actually went to war our essential demands had already been met.

By this time, however, the yellow press had another case for incitement to war, in the explosion which had sunk our battleship, *The Maine*, in Havana harbor. This disaster was laid at the door of Spain, even though it had almost surely not been caused by Spain. The press howled for war to avenge the national honor.

The administration of President McKinley bowed, at last, to a basic rule of politics: where you cannot lead you had better follow. It had tried, like its predecessor, to calm public opinion and to achieve a diplomatic settlement with Spain before too late. Now it saw an excited Congress, moved by the mass emotion, preparing to act on its own to have a war. It fell into step and, two days after the Spanish capitulation to our demands, the President sent his war message to Congress.

Historians and statesmen since Thucydides have recognized, as a prime danger inherent in war, that states which embark on it tend to lose control of their own destiny. A typical manifestation of this danger is the repeated inability of states to keep to the limited objectives for which they have gone to war, once victory comes

within their reach. Our war with Spain had the sole objective of liberating Cuba. This objective was made explicit in a joint Congressional resolution which disclaimed territorial greed by foreswearing any disposition to acquire Cuba for ourselves.

As we now know, Spain did not have the military means to defend Cuba. We might therefore have confined our military effort to the vicinity of Cuba, making the military objective the same as the political objective, that of pulling Cuba out of the Spanish grasp. There was really no more necessity of attacking Spain's islands in the Pacific than of attacking her islands in the Mediterranean. Military orthodoxy since Clausewitz, however, has held that the prime military objective in warfare (or in warfare at its best) is not the capture of territory but the destruction of the enemy's power and will to fight. Since our military had been brought up on this doctrine it did not occur to them to limit or localize the military effort. It would surely have been hard to show them any reason for doing so.

For many decades we had maintained a small naval squadron in the western Pacific, apparently to support our commerce and "show the flag." Commodore Dewey's predecessor in command of that squadron, seeing the likelihood of war with Spain and knowing that a Spanish naval squadron was roosting in the Philippines, made plans for an attack on that squadron, plans which Commodore Dewey inherited from him. Such action by a naval officer in such a position is less noteworthy, perhaps, than would have been its omission.

In a real sense, no positive decision ever was taken to adopt a policy calling for an attack on the Philippines. The President merely found that this was the naval policy that the navy had in mind, and he seems to have assumed that it must be right. "While we remained at war with Spain," Dewey later wrote, "our purpose must be to strike at the power of Spain wherever possible." This implication of unlimited war, which might have given a Bismarck pause, was unquestioned among us at the time. The *political* objective of the war was to liberate Cuba; but the *military* objective must be to hurt Spain wherever we could until she cried quits. The western Pacific was one of the principal places where we could hurt her. Given these premises, the naval officers were right in assuming that we would strike at the Philippines in case of war. A special policy decision would have been needed rather to exempt them from the area of our military operations than to include them.

The outbreak of war did not, in itself, occasion the dispatch of any orders whatever to Commodore Dewey, who lay in Britain's colony of Hong Kong with our Far Eastern squadron. Action to instruct him on what he should do was taken only in response to an urgent cable from him, reporting that the British declaration of neutrality forced him to leave Hong Kong immediately and requesting instructions. At a meeting in the White House an order to Dewey was drafted and the President approved it. It read: "War has commenced. . . .Proceed at once to Philippine Islands. Commence operations particularly against the Spanish fleet. You must capture vessels or destroy. Use utmost endeavor." No one thought of this order in terms of the significance that it might have for the general position of the United States in the Far East. It represented merely the implementation of a war strategy that had never been questioned.

Dewey carried out his mission with punctilio and daring. He proceeded to the Bay of Manila, where the Spanish squadron lay, and destroyed it at its anchorage without the loss of a single American life.

The American people had been showing increasing frustration at the lack of any heroic military action coincident with the outbreak of war, and the government in Washington had been coming under mounting criticism for timidity. Dewey's departure from Hong Kong and his destination were front-page news on April 25. For five tense days nothing more was heard. Then, on May 2, the news of the victory came. The relief and rejoicing were universal, but no place more so, I suspect, than in the corridors of Washington where the public pressure for action had been so keenly felt. A *New York Times* dispatch reporting this added: "The victory has scarcely been fully reported before the fact flashes upon the Administration, as it has upon the European diplomatic circles, that the United States Government has suddenly acquired a status in the East that was not at all looked for, and that may greatly change the discussion of Eastern problems." This is not the last time. . .that we shall have occasion to note how implications of an event that become obvious immediately after it takes place remain unforeseen throughout the period in which it is anticipated only.

Until this moment, no one in Washington had concerned himself with the implications and consequences of Dewey's mission. No one had asked: What next? Consequently, when the Spanish squadron had been destroyed Dewey found himself without those landing forces which he would need to carry out the "offensive operations in Philippines" that he had been instructed to undertake after dealing with the squadron. This omission also became obvious to Washington in the moment of victory.

Although Dewey himself was not heard from until May 7, on May 3 the Commanding General of the Army recommended to the Secretary of War that General Thomas M. Anderson be sent "to occupy the Philippine Islands," in command of certain specified troops; and on May 4 the President ordered that these troops be assembled at San Francisco. This represented the decision, made without forethought, to take the Philippines, whether temporarily or permanently.

Still, no one was clear on the mission of these landing forces. The general chosen to command them, having had an interview with the President on May 12, wrote him on the 15th: "I do not yet know whether it is your desire to subdue and hold all of the Spanish territory in the islands, or merely to seize and hold the capital." The President didn't know either. Finally, however, on May 19 he defined the mission of the expeditionary force in a letter to the Secretary of War. He wrote that: "The destruction of the Spanish fleet at Manila, followed by the taking of the naval station at Cavite, the paroling of the garrisons, and acquisition of the control of the bay, have rendered it necessary, in the further prosecution of the measures adopted by this Government for the purpose of bringing about an honorable and durable peace with Spain, to send an army of occupation to the Philippines for the twofold purpose of completing the reduction of the Spanish power in that quarter and of giving order and security to the islands while in the possession of the United States. . . .

"The first effect of the military occupation of the enemy's territory is the severance of the former political relations of the inhabitants and the establishment of a new political power. . . ."

Without looking forward as far as the postwar future, but merely trying to stay abreast of the present, the government had concluded that events "rendered it necessary" to take possession of the Philippine Islands.

At this time the American people had shown themselves thoroughly opposed to the acquisition of overseas territory even as close in as the Hawaiian Islands. Consequently, no one, at first, contemplated the possibility that the Philippines might be kept in our possession. To some it seemed that we should hold them as collateral for a Spanish indemnity at the war's end, returning them to Spain upon its payment. To others it seemed logical that we should grant them their independence, as we intended to do with Cuba.

The mental uncertainty and agony which the *New York Times* displayed on its editorial page is representative. On May 3 it found it unthinkable that we should ever return the islands to Spain. Exploring alternatives, it added that "nobody pretends that the natives of the Philippines are fit for self-government, as we believe the Cubans to be. On the other hand, all the arguments against the annexation of Hawaii are available, with even greater force, against our retention of the Philippines for ourselves." It concluded that we had already incurred a responsibility in seizing them which could be discharged only by having Great Britain take them off our hands.

The following day, in one and the same editorial, the *Times* was saying that "we could not in any event take the islands for ourselves," and also that if Britain "declines to take them on reasonable terms we must even retain them for ourselves," since we could neither return them to Spain nor hand them over to their primitive inhabitant. It was thus foreseeing the possibility of a dilemma in which every possible alternative was impossible to contemplate—such a dilemma as is not unique in the conduct of foreign affairs.

Finally, by May 9, the *Times* had at last brought itself to contemplate what could not be contemplated at first. "It is becoming plainer every day," it said, "that paramount necessity will compel us to assume for a time of which we cannot now see the end the duty of governing and controlling the Philippine Islands."

The President, too, was still behind the march of events, trying to catch up with them. Being at a loss to know what we should do with the Philippines, now that they were at our disposal, he postponed decision. One of the conditions that he made for a truce with beaten Spain, on July 30, was that we should continue to occupy "the city, bay and harbor of Manila pending the conclusion of a treaty of peace which shall determine the control, disposition, and the government of the Philippines."

At last, on September 16, in his instructions to the American commissioners appointed to negotiate the peace with Spain, the President wrote: "Without any original thought of complete or even partial acquisition, the presence and success of our arms at Manila imposes upon us obligations which we cannot disregard. The march of events rules and overrules human action. . . .we cannot be unmindful that without any desire or design on our part the war has brought us new duties and responsibilities which we must meet and discharge as becomes a great nation on whose growth and career from the beginning the Ruler of Nations has plainly written the high command and pledge of civilization."

We may not doubt that President McKinley, who sought divine guidance for his decision on the Philippines, wrote this with sincerity. But it confronts us with a paradox that goes to the root of this inquiry. It virtually states, in its first two sentences, that "the presence and success of our arms at Manila" does not belong in the category of "human action" but in some other category that "overrules human action." This other category is identified with "the march of events." Here the government of the United States discounts its own authority over the march of events, conceding the sway of destiny.

President McKinley, unhappily deciding at last that we had no choice but to make the Philippines ours, concluded that destiny must have predetermined an outcome so far from our intentions. This immediately became the view of all who faced the unexpected consequence of Dewey's famous victory at Manila Bay. Captain Alfred Thayer Mahan, who had participated notably in the development of the strategy which led to Dewey's victory, wrote: ". . .the preparation made for us, rather than by us, in the unwilling acquisition of the Philippines, is so obvious as to embolden even the least presumptuous to see in it the hand of Providence."

Surely, however, it was by actions of our own free choice that we at last found ourselves holding the Philippines. Surely we had been free to shape our policy so that we would not acquire them. Surely it was by our own decision that the Philippines came into our hands.

In point of fact, there never was a decision to attach the Philippines to us until it was found that they virtually were attached already. By the time the issue was full-blown, the question which presented itself for decision was not whether we should *take* them. It was whether we should *keep* them. And by this time there was no acceptable alternative to keeping them.

ROBERT E. OSGOOD (1921-   ), Director of the
Washington Center for Foreign Policy Research and a
frequent commentator on American foreign policy, argues,
unlike LaFeber, that the McKinley Administration did not
enter the Spanish-American War as a result of calculations
designed to gain any national advantage. He views the war
as motivated by idealism stemming from American
Protestantism combined with romanticis n and national
egoism as exemplified by such political figures as Alfred
Thayer Mahan and Theodore Roosevelt. Osgood, like
George F. Kennan, believes that one of the most serious
problems of American foreign policy since the late
nineteenth century has been that of reconciling the
country's idealistic traditions with national self-interest.
But any estimate of the wisdom of McKinley's expansionist
policies must attempt to answer the following question:
what kind of foreign policy would have represented a
proper balance between idealism and national self-interest
during 1898-1899?°

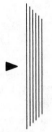

Ideals and Self-interest
in Foreign Policy

It was the Spanish-American War which
brought the American people to the full
consciousness of their power in the world.
For a decade before that event Mahan and
his followers had been realistically charting
the shifting currents of international politics and setting the course of national aggrandizement accordingly. But there was
little in the impact of power politics upon
the lay mind to suggest that the general
public respected Mahan's chart, no matter
how keenly they shared his eagerness for
the voyage. That the American people were
off on a great adventure was clear to all, but
whether they knew where they were going
or would understand where they were
when they had arrived seemed doubtful, if
one could judge from the complacency, the
capricious nationalism, and the light-
hearted moral assurance of the nineties.

When one realizes how little relation the
origin of America's war with Spain had with
its consequences, it is easy to understand
how historians conclude that an Unseen
Hand or some great impersonal force, like
geography or economics, determines the
course of nations. Indeed, the United States
displayed much of the facility of the mother
country for acquiring an empire in a fit of
absent-mindedness. Americans began the
war not out of a realistic calculation of national advantage but largely as an idealistic
crusade to free the Cubans from Spain's
imperial shackles. Yet they ended it with a

°Reprinted from Robert E. Osgood, *Ideals and Self Interest in America's Foreign Relations* (Chicago: The
University of Chicago Press, 1953), pp. 42-57. Copyright 1953 by The University of Chicago. Reprinted by
permission of the publisher. Footnotes omitted.

far-flung empire of their own from the Philippines to Hawaii to Puerto Rico. They undertook the war as a local action, but their victory affected the relations among all the great powers of the world.

As in all crusades, idealism was not unmixed with other motives. Not before or since the Spanish-American War have the American people experienced such a paroxysm of national pride and chauvinism. Clearly, they were ripe for the event. The United States had had no foreign war since 1848. It had fully recovered from the Civil War and just surmounted the panic of 1893. The mighty nations of the world were restless, and Americans were anxious to have a suitable role in the world drama that seemed about to commence. America had stuck her toe into the turbulent waters of imperialism during the Samoan adventure, had taken a hasty dip when the Harrison administration just missed annexing Hawaii, and had boldly splashed Great Britain with Cleveland's ultimatum during the Venezuela crisis. In 1898 she was ready to take the big plunge.

However, the public as a whole, as distinguished from its more nationalistic, navy-minded, or power-conscious members was not ready to take the plunge just for the sheer joy of getting wet. That would have been inconsistent with the American tradition of refraining from intervention in other people's affairs, of decrying aggression and acquisitiveness. But the pitiful plight of the Cuban revolutionists was a different matter. A war to free Cuba from Spanish despotism, corruption, and cruelty, from the filth and disease and barbarity of General "Butcher" Weyler's reconcentration camps, from the devastation of haciendas, the extermination of families, and the outraging of women; that would be a blow for humanity and democracy. No one could doubt it if he believed—and

skepticism was not popular—the exaggerations of the Cuban *Junta's* propaganda and the lurid distortions and imaginative lies purveyed by the "yellow sheets" of Hearst and Pulitzer at the combined rate of two million a day.

Yet it took the melodramatic explosion of the American battleship *Maine* in Havana Harbor with the loss of 260 American seamen to precipitate war. Although succeeding years have yielded little credible evidence that the Spanish were responsible for the sinking, Americans were in no mood for sifting evidence at the time. The public pressure generated by the ensuing emotional outburst swept away all reason and hesitation. Apparently, the incident ignited the spark of chauvinism that was needed to fire humanitarian sentiment to war heat.

However, it was not humanly possible for the excitement of that fateful spring of 1898 to last long once war had set in. As passion waned, outraged humanitarianism gave way to a broader idealism, and frenzied jingoism was supplanted by a general sense of national power and destiny. Yet when the war of liberation assumed the proportions of extensive conquest, an increasing number of Americans found that even this milder combination of moral enthusiasm and national self-assertiveness failed to recommend itself to reason or conscience. The Spanish-American War was, as wars go, remarkably brief and painless, and many enjoyed it almost as much as Theodore Roosevelt; but even before it ended, voices of doubt and dissent were raised. Less than a decade later, Americans had lost interest in the plight of the Cubans and all the other alien peoples for whose regeneration the nation had fought; and a great many citizens, especially those devoted to the growing peace movement, looked upon Hay's "splended little war" as the very antithesis of idealism. They were inclined to agree with the anti-imperialists of 1900 that the nation's better instincts had fallen prey to sheer power lust, that its profession of an ideal mission had been the hypocritical pretense of individual and collective greed or, at best, a transparent rationalization of national aggressiveness. And the fact that some of the most critical anti-imperialists, like William Jennings Bryan, had been in the vanguard of the crusaders added the poignancy of disillusionment to the passion of self-righteousness.

The animadversions of anti-imperialists notwithstanding, there was nothing cynical about the way America embarked on its capricious crusade. McKinley was very much the voice of the people when he said of Cuba in his annual message of 1897, "I speak not of forcible annexation, for that can not be thought of. That by our code of morality would be criminal aggression." The joint resolution which declared that the United States would free Cuba also disclaimed, in the Teller Amendment, any intention of annexing Cuba. This provision was unanimously approved in Congress, and so far as anyone has been able to tell, approved by the great majority of the public as well.

According to a popular assumption in the years following the war, America was drawn into the war by businessmen in search of new markets and investment opportunities. But, actually, businessmen, far from perpetrating the war, were, except for a few who made a living off Cuban investment and trade, generally more reluctant than most citizens to disturb the ordinary pattern of peace and commerce; they were largely opposed or indifferent to the selfish, material aspects of the enterprise until the acquisition of the Philippines raised great hopes of new markets. If any interest group, aside from the Navy, can be singled out for its special enthusiasm for going forth to battle, it is Protestantism, which was deeply impressed by Spanish

inhumanity and the opportunities for missionary activity in the Orient.

It may be that moral principles were espoused, in part, as a rationalization of nationalistic conceit and avarice. But idealistic professions were no flimsy fabrication or afterthought; they were the product of a compelling conviction, rooted solidly in American character and tradition. It was a combination of idealism and egoism, of knight-errantry and national self-assertiveness, that moved the American people to support military action; and one motive was as important as the other.

It cannot be doubted that some highly articulate publicists saw in a war to liberate Cuba a providential opportunity to enact their program of national glory. These men composed that small coterie of nationalist politicians, naval strategists, and scholars who, for a decade or more, had led the preparedness and expansionist movements. Sea power, new markets, new investment opportunities, protection of trade routes, territorial expansion—all these objects were bound up with a genuine missionary zeal, but, as far as Mahan, Roosevelt, Lodge, and Albert J. Beveridge were concerned, they were probably sufficient reasons in themselves for meeting the moribund Spanish Empire in battle. Mahan saw the Spanish-American War as "something of a side issue." Theodore Roosevelt thought it would be "good for the Navy." The war looked like a magnificent opportunity to gain popular support for the powerful fleet essential to a larger commercial and political future. Mahan and Beveridge were about the only expansionists who advocated intervention as a means of commercial development, but economic considerations were an integral part of the gospel of naval strength, strategic territories, and the extension of American influence in the world. All these objects of national aggrandizement had been in the forefront of ultranationalist minds during the abortive attempt to annex Hawaii; the same men looked forward to a war with Spain as another chance to make good. They welcomed the Spanish-American War as a supreme opportunity to enact Mahan's whole strategic program of dominant bases in the Caribbean, an Isthmian canal, and the development of a Pacific frontier.

To be sure, the men who composed the nucleus of the expansionist agitation yielded to no one in their affirmation of moral purpose. Several months before the sinking of the *Maine*, Roosevelt privately advocated a war to lift the burden from the wretched Cubans, and even when urging this project before naval men, he did not fail to place considerations of humanity ahead of naval and strategic considerations. However, it is significant that this undoubtedly sincere idealism was not the kind that called for a restraint upon national egoism but rather the kind that demanded a vigorous assertion of the national will; and the closer to war Roosevelt came, the less he restrained his self-assertive egoism. In his private correspondence just before the outbreak of war he gave humanitarian and broad idealistic considerations about equal weight with arguments for the national self-interest, which called for avenging American honor and establishing American bases in the Caribbean; but by the time he was on board the ship off Florida that would carry him and his Rough Riders to high adventure in Cuba, he was urging Lodge to prevent any talk of peace until the United States got Manila, Hawaii, Puerto Rico, and the Philippines.

When Roosevelt sent Admiral Dewey to the little-known Philippine Islands, and Dewey dramatized the sudden extension of the conflict by annihilating a decrepit Spanish fleet in Manila Harbor, the expansionists' humanitarian exertions began to embrace more ambitious goals, their missionary fervor converged with a swelling urge for national power, their idealism merged with bellicosity. Albert J. Beveridge struck this note early in his famous imperialist pronouncement before the Middlesex Club of Boston, in which, just two days after the formal declaration of war, he proclaimed its objectives as expansion. The acquisition of new markets and new lands, Beveridge said, was "part of the Almighty's infinite plan, the disappearance of debased civilizations and decaying races before the higher civilization of the nobler and more virile types of men." He was frank in his avowal of material self-interest: "American factories are making more than the American people can use; American soil is producing more than they can consume. Fate has written our policy for us; the trade of the world must and shall be ours." But he did not neglect the missionary aspects of expansion: "And American law, American order, American civilization, and the American flag will plant themselves on shores hitherto bloody and benighted, but by those agencies of God henceforth to be made beautiful and bright."

It is important to recognize the pugnacious instincts which underlay the exhortations of these nationalistic spokesmen, because the aggressive quality of their imperialism explains much about the popular reception of their views in the years that followed the war with Spain. Beveridge, like Mahan, believed in the beneficent influence of national aggressiveness upon the progress of civilization. He decried the loss of moral fiber that comes from the sterile pursuit of material pleasures. Through great deeds, he proclaimed, the nation must evoke a sense of religious dedication in its citizens, lest it spawn a generation of self-centered weaklings and spineless money-grubbers. Strong nations make strong men. The qualities Beveridge admired in men were the qualities he admired in nations: courage, energy, masterfulness. He was "obsessed with the thought of empire building, of redeeming waste places, of subduing inferior peoples to the will of the master nations, of maintaining order, setting up the machinery of civilization."

Theodore Roosevelt made himself a living example of the virile, fighting qualities, the martial virtues, the strenuous life. And as he despised "mollycoddles," so he abhorred timidity in nations. A nation, like an individual, he believed, must always deal squarely and champion righteousness; but, above all, it must be saturated with a fierce concern for its rights and its honor; and just as an honorable man must on occasion resort to fisticuffs, so an honorable nation must go to war. War held no horrors for Roosevelt. In 1886 he was elated by the prospect of a good scrap in Mexico and offered to organize his Medora ranch hands into a cavalry battalion. In 1892 he dreamed of leading a cavalry charge to enforce the United States demands that Chile pay an indemnity for injuries American sailors had incurred in a Valparaiso brawl. In 1895 he welcomed a war with Great Britain in defense of America's right to demand arbitration of the Venezuela boundary dispute, and he thought that the United States might well conquer Canada while it was about it. When the Spanish-American War erupted, Roosevelt was haunted by the fear that it might end before he got into it.

Although love of violence may be one incentive for seriously regarding the imperatives of national power, it can be readily seen that there was much in the imperialist and expansionist rationale, especially in its martial code of virility and honor, which had no logical relation to a realistic view of world politics. This rationale would seem to have been chiefly the product of a strong temperamental or emotional bias against idealism and its values of love, reason, humility, and self-denial. In many respects American imperialism of the 1890's echoed the yea-saying of the nineteenth-century romantic rebellion against the tame virtues of utilitarianism and individualism, against the Age of Enlightenment and its middle-class values. The spirit of imperialism was an exaltation of duty above rights, of collective welfare above individual self-interest, the heroic values as opposed to materialism, action instead of logic, the natural impulse rather than the pallid intellect. This romantic Weltanschauung, which possessed Mahan and Roosevelt and other egoistic Realists, goes a long way to explain the unfriendly reception which the American public accorded their views on foreign relations after the war.

The Growth of Anti-Imperialism

Undoubtedly, combative instincts were less highly developed in the general American public than in Roosevelt or Beveridge. Few could have been so eager to save their manliness at the risk of losing their lives at this juncture in the history of warfare. Yet something of the imperialists' truculence did seize the American people and fill them with a desire to show the world that the United States had come into its own. A perceptive editorial in the *Washington Post* described the new sensation:

A new consciousness seems to have come upon us—the consciousness of strength—and with it a new appetite, the yearning to show our strength. It might be compared with the effect upon the animal creation of the taste of blood.

Ambition, interest, land hunger, pride, the mere joy of fighting, whatever it may be, we are animated by a new sensation. We are face to face with a strange destiny.

The taste of empire is in the mouth of the people even as the taste of blood in the jungle. It means an imperial policy, the Republic renascent, taking her place with the armed nations.

The United States was not long in tasting its first imperial blood, but the after-taste was not so pleasant as the first sampling; for when hostilities ended, less than four months after they had begun, the American people suddenly found themselves arguing about what they should do with the Philippines and its liberated inhabitants. Once the fighting was over, most Americans, having an ordinary susceptibility to the temptations of peace and harmony, found less incentive for bellicosity; and some began to wonder if national glory were sufficient compensation for the unwonted task of supervising an alien people on the other side of the Pacific Ocean, especially at the risk of embroiling the nation in the quarrelsome arena of world politics.

To be sure, imperialists advanced weighty moral reasons for assuming the burden of empire. They argued that the United States had a solemn obligation to sustain the liberating and civilizing mission it had set out to fulfil. And even when this mission encountered the armed resistance of its beneficiaries, the advocates of empire, confirmed in their opinion that the Filipinos were incapable of self-government, urged Americans, in the words of Kipling's timely poem, to "take up the white man's burden" for the sake of the true interests of the misguided heathens.

But, as the war spirit abated, the imperialists' interpretation of ideals became less and less persuasive. Their willingness to govern an alien people without its consent and then to meet its dissent with bullets; their unwillingness to renounce permanent sovereignty or even to establish a protectorate; the contrast between the original aims of the war and these practical consequences, together with their openly avowed predilections toward violence; these circumstances suggested to those with less agressive temperaments and more sensitive consciences that the promoters of American destiny were guilty of flagrant inconsistency, if not outright deceit, in their professions of altruism.

By the time the debate on the disposition of the Philippines reached its peak, the imperialist assertion of a Manifest Destiny which mere mortals were powerless to resist had begun to sound less like the rallying cry for a crusade then the whimpering alibi for a morally dubious venture. The growth of anti-imperialist sentiment among political leaders as well as among literary figures, journalists, social reformers, and intellectuals promised at least to embarrass Destiny even if it could not halt it.

The anti-imperialist movement, in its inception, was pre-eminently a moral protest. Focusing upon America's rule—and, later, subjugation—of alien peoples against their will and contrary to the principles upon which the nation was founded, the anti-imperialists drew upon all the hallowed principles of liberty and humanitarianism for which Americans prided themselves in order to expose imperialism as an evil distortion of the original purpose of the war and a travesty upon the national mission. America, they protested, had undertaken the war as a liberator, not as a conqueror. As for her mission of regenerating the world, which the imperialists invoked, they insisted that its achievement depended upon the power of example, not the might of the sword. In fact, they regarded imperialism as the very denial of America's mission, for how could the nation exemplify love and justice while engaged in aggrandizement and coercion? "No, do not deceive yourselves," cried Carl Schurz.

If we turn that war which was so solemnly

commended to the favor of mankind as a generous war of liberation and humanity into a victory for conquest and self-aggrandizement, we shall have thoroughly forfeited our moral credit with the world. Professions of unselfish virtue and benevolence, proclamations of noble humanitarian purposes coming from us will never, never be trusted again.

Although Carl Schurz and his fellow anti-imperialists were, at first, but a narrow protest group sniping at the moral outposts of entrenched imperialism, they fought with the complete assurance that they were on the side of the Lord and the Declaration of Independence; and, in the end, the imperialists proved no match for the spiritual might of their zealous adversaries. Indeed, the superior moral confidence of the anti-imperialists was not misplaced, for they were squarely in line with America's deep-rooted liberal and humane tradition. They took as their text the American Creed, the whole heritage of Enlightenment embodied in American nationalism, the ingrained pattern of idealism permeating the national thought and speech, the pervasive belief in the dignity and perfectibility of man, the sacred postulates of freedom and justice enshrined in the maxims of the national gods and heroes. In the light of these principles, the imperialist fulminations about virility, destiny, and the white man's burden seemed like a reversion to the discredited doctrines of militarism and acquisitiveness, which America had renounced when she severed her ties with the Old World and established a better way of life in the New.

These moral protestations struck some Realists as the product of an extremely silly view of international relations. What could one expect from war? In their minds there was something incongruous about playing the devil's game for heavenly stakes. Yet some of the prominent "ultrapacifists," whom Mahan and Roosevelt denounced,

had been the strongest advocates of a holy war. Perhaps the anti-imperialists, and the American people in general, had set the stakes of war too high; but they were new to the game, and once they were in it, it was too late to renege.

In retrospect it seems evident that this war could have retained the support of American idealists and anti-imperialists only if it could have been reconciled with traditional principles of progress and the national mission, principles for which men like Bryan had supported the crusade in the first place. Unlike the imperialists, these men could reconcile themselves to the violence of war only through the highest moral expectations. But could any war possibly fulfil such expectations? For that matter, could any national policy, violent or peaceful, effective or ineffective, avoid the contradictions and compromises with perfection which the idealists of 1898 chose to ignore?

The impact of the Spanish-American War upon sensitive consciences is more comprehensible when one realizes the abhorrence with which many idealists in the nineties—particularly the evangelical pacifists, liberal intellectuals, and reformers—looked upon war itself. It was a singular circumstance that at the very time the nation thrilled to its greatest surge of aggressive nationalism it was also feeling a new hopefulness and enthusiasm for the abolition of war. The growing number of international conferences, arbitrations, conciliations, and mediations throughout the world, the beginnings of a democratic renaissance at home, and the spread of humanitarianism and social reform suggested to the more progressive elements of society that a new day was dawning in international relations. The growing power of the people was believed to guarantee the ultimate triumph of justice over greed and special privilege, among nations as well as among classes, while the spread of humanitarianism and the increasing tendency to resolve social conflicts by reason instead of force seemed to presage the gradual disappearance of armaments, secret diplomacy, and all the other sources of national conflict dividing man from man. Some were even permitted to hope that in their lifetimes the scourge of war would follow the anachronistic practice of the duel into oblivion.

For those who shared these high hopes and ideals, the only compelling justification, other than self-defense, for the United States, of all nations, to resort to war was the advancement of Christianity, democracy, and humanitarianism. Consequently, when their crusade degenerated into conquest, the indignation which moral optimists poured upon the imperialists reflected the bitterness of remorse as well as the consciousness of thwarted expectations.

Self-interest in the Debate over Empire

As the great debate over imperialism reached its climax in the Presidential campaign of 1900, it clearly revealed its origin in basically conflicting attitudes toward international relations. The trend of that debate shows that the controversy between imperialists and anti-imperialists turned as much upon differing conceptions of national self-interest as upon divergent interpretations of the American mission.

In the course of the struggle the imperialists met their antagonists' moral assault by falling back upon more familiar positions. As the force of circumstances and the growing opposition of the anti-imperialists began to cast doubt upon the idealistic professions of imperialism, the proponents of expansion and empire shifted the emphasis of their arguments toward the selfish national advantage. They began to say more about evidence of the islands' economic and strategic value, about their vital function in preserving a foothold in the highly competitive markets of the Far East, and about the folly of abandoning them to the predatory instincts of Japan and Germany.

Indeed there were valid considerations of political and strategic advantage which weighed heavily in the decision to keep all the Philippines. That decision cannot be understood solely in terms of President McKinley's famous account of divine guidance, which he delivered to a group of visiting clergymen. At the end of the war the configuration of international power in the world and the alignment of national interests in the Pacific were such that, had the United States given the Filipinos immediate independence, with the great risk of plunging them into anarchy, the great powers—particularly Germany, Japan, England, and Russia—would almost certainly have been tempted to intervene. This would have touched off a scramble for position that might well have precipitated a world war, from which the United States could hardly have remained isolated.

However, these strategic considerations actually played a small role in the public arguments of the imperialists. That Realists, who certainly appreciated them privately, should have given them so little publicity is, perhaps, an indication of their recognition of the American public's indifference or antipathy toward power politics. Instead, they presented their self-interested arguments for empire in terms of emotional appeals to American prestige and honor. The thought of surrendering a prize of war was obviously repugnant to the imperialists' sense of national self-exaltation. Such a sacrifice of patent self-interest for the sake of a dubious moral gesture struck the nationalistic mind as a futile and dangerous species of unrealism and softness. And so President McKinley, Senator Lodge, Whitelaw Reid, ex-Minister Charles Denby, and others fervently warned against hauling down the flag and rendering Americans an object of derision among the power-wise nations of the world.

What the imperialists were saying, fundamentally, was that national idealism was contingent; that it was valid only as long as it was not inconsistent with national self-interest. And in their view America's self-interest inhered chiefly in her reputation amid the society of great nations for excelling in the competitive struggle for military strength and commercial predominance. There was no need for making this hard-headed premise of international politics explicit as long as America's crusading ardor was at a high pitch, but when it showed signs of faltering, imperialists felt that it was necessary to elucidate the more compelling bases of national conduct.

Thus in the early stages of the debate over Philippine independence Senator Lodge was willing to meet idealists on their own ground. "The opponents of the treaty have placed their opposition on such high and altruistic grounds that I have preferred to meet them there." But as imperialists and anti-imperialists marshaled their forces for the election campaign of 1900, he made it clear that, in his mind, national interest would always take precedence over conflicting international altruism. Philanthropy was all right, but philanthropy at the expense of American power and prestige was akin to suicide, in Lodge's opinion. In a speech before the Republican National Convention he stated the case for hard-headedness very simply: "We make no hypocritical pretense of being interested in the Philippines solely on account of others. While we regard the welfare of these people as a sacred trust, we regard the welfare of the American people first."

In the same year Richard Olney, formerly Secretary of State under President Cleveland and an astute observer of the changing scene, published an article in the *Atlantic Monthly*, which, although it turned Lodge's argument back upon the imperialists by criticizing the purchase of the Philippines as contrary to the national interest, nevertheless succeeded in expressing the realistic view of the relation of idealism and self-interest more succinctly than the imperialists themselves. Olney deprecated the sickly sentimentality that had led the United States to regard the acquisition and pacification of the Philippines as a humanitarian enterprise. The paramount of duty of a government, he declared, is to its own subjects; benevolence and charity are simply incidental and subsidiary. This was in the nature of things, and must be the policy of every power.

> None can afford not to attend strictly to its own business and not to make the welfare of its own people its primary object—none can afford to regard itself as a sort of missionary nation charged with the rectification of errors and the redress of wrongs the world over. Were the United States to enter upon its new international role with the serious purpose of carrying out any such theory, it would not merely be laughed at but voted a nuisance by all other nations—and treated accordingly.

The difference between Olney and the imperialistic Realists lay not in their understanding of the role of self-interest in national conduct but in their conceptions of what kind of self-interest America ought to pursue. Olney argued that the acquisition of the Philippines was contrary to American self-interest because it would unnecessarily entangle the nation in the world struggle for commercial and political supremacy, enfeeble it with the burden of defending an immense, remote, and vulnerable area, and bring no material benefits in return; but the imperialists were not content to define national self-interest as mere material welfare, comfort, and security; they were thinking in bolder terms of self-assertion and self-aggrandizement.

Yet it is significant that, as it rapidly became evident after the acquisition of the Philippines that America's new charges might be a literal and not just a romantic burden, some of the leading imperialists seem to have been troubled with doubts about the priority of their heroic conception of self-interest over Olney's more prosaic view. These doubts could be only partially resolved by devotion to the moral responsibility and duty of fulfilling the American mission. Thus Roosevelt, who less than a decade later was calling the Philippines America's "achilles heel," wrote to Frederic Coudert in 1901,

While I have never varied in my feeling that we had to hold the Philippines, I have varied very much in my feelings whether we were to be considered fortunate or unfortunate in having to hold them, and I most earnestly hope that the trend of events will as speedily as may be justify us in leaving them. . . . Sometimes I feel that it is an intensely disagreeable and unfortunate task which we cannot in honor shirk. At other times I am tempted to think that the whole business fits in with my favorite doctrine, and that we should count ourselves fortunate in having a great work to do.

Roosevelt's doubts were but a pale reflection of the doubts that seized the nation as a whole. They foreboded the collapse of the imperialist counterattack. To the majority of Americans the imperialists' appeal to national self-interest seemed increasingly dubious on both ethical and practical grounds.

If opponents of expansion and empire were more sensitive to the moral issue than imperialists, their position was no less governed by a conception of national interest. They charged that annexation of the Philippines would be contrary not only to democratic principles and international ethics but also to the American tradition of nonin-

terference and nonentanglement in world politics. They were afraid that the acquisition of an empire would not only destroy the United States' moral position in the world but would also expose Americans to endless foreign wars and saddle them with the loss of liberty and the expense that would accompany the maintenance of a large military establishment. As the distinguished Yale scholar William Graham Sumner expressed it in his powerful indictment, *The Conquest of the United States by Spain*, "Expansion and imperialism are at war with the best traditions, principles, and interests of the American people, and . . . they will plunge us into a network of difficult problems and political perils which we might have avoided, while they offer us no corresponding advantage in return."

Political and social reformers, like Carl Schurz, Moorfield Storey, and E. L. Godkin, and liberal-minded intellectuals, like David Starr Jordan, William James, Charles Eliot Norton, Mark Twain, and William Dean Howells, attributed America's moral prestige, the progress of her democratic government, and her marvelous material development in large part to her relative isolation from the turbulent affairs of European nations. These men were not impressed by Mahan's prophecies of economic and strategic advantages. To them the white man's burden meant the ordeal of governing an ignorant and hostile people, while embroiling the nation in a contest for foreign markets, territorial aggrandizement, and ever larger armaments.

The Rationalization of Self-interest

In some respects the great debate over imperialism sounded like *Alice in Wonderland*. Both sides used the same words, but the words seemed to mean different things. Imperialists and anti-imperialists alike proclaimed, with equal sincerity no doubt, their faith in America's mission, the spread of liberty, and the regeneration of mankind. Yet, although both groups had generally supported America's crusade at its inception, each later charged the other with subverting it, while asserting that it alone remained true to the national ideals.

The pervasiveness and uniformity of the idea of the American mission suggest that divergent attitudes toward national self-interest were the controlling factor in the conflict between imperialists and their antagonists, even when the controversy was cast in ideal terms. In the imperialist view the self-interest of the nation lay in a positive assertion of national power in accordance with a Manifest Destiny of world dominion. This view was consistent with a pugnacious, aggressive attitude and a temperamental bias toward heroic action and the military virtues. Anti-imperialists, on the other hand, conceived of national self-interest as the preservation of the status quo in accordance with the wisdom of the Forefathers, a conception which was consonant with a more pacific disposition, an exaltation of reason and love, and an aversion toward violence.

In response to a primary characteristic of national sentiment, not to say the propensity of all human beings for rationalizing their self-interest, patriots of both imperialist and anti-imperialist persuasion sought to identify the selfish interest of the nation, as they saw it, with ideal purposes. Consequently, their particular views of national interest and their proclivities somewhat colored their interpretations of the traditional American mission. Thus imperialists found that commercial and territorial expansion, no matter how the consequences might affect its alleged beneficiaries, were truly instruments of civilization and democracy; and they were confident that the full exercise of man's com-

bative instincts in the competitive struggle of nations was the best assurance of America's moral fiber and the vitality of American principles. Anti-imperialists, on the other hand, asserted that the fulfillment of America's exalted mission depended upon her continued isolation from the vicissitudes of world politics, since only by remaining politically detached from the controversies and combinations of European powers could the nation remain faithful to Washington's advice and "give to mankind the magnanimous and too novel example of a people always guided by an exalted justice and benevolence."

As might be expected, each side charged the other with selfishness. Imperialists asserted that the tradition of isolation was selfish because it thwarted the moral ambition of the nation out of a mean and narrow concern for mere safety from the hazards of international politics. Anti-imperialists denounced their antagonists for abandoning principle in the service of greed, for sacrificing America's moral reputation to an inordinate lust for power. But, actually, neither the imperialist nor anti-imperialist view was wholly selfish or wholly idealistic. The important difference between the two camps lay, first, in their conception of national self-interest and, secondly, in the way they combined self-interest with ideal purpose.

Obviously, aggressive national egoism is more likely to conflict with the interests of other peoples than passive national egoism. Therefore, an attitude of self-assertiveness, unlike an attitude of self-denial, tends to become incongruous with liberal and humane principles. It is in this situation that patriots are confronted with the problem of consciously reconciling national self-interest with supranational ideals. American imperialists solved the problem, to their own satisfaction, not by disavowing ideals but by relegating them to a secondary status. When the vicissitudes of empire and the moral strictures of anti-imperialists centered public attention upon the growing incompatibility of a robust national egoism with international altruism, some of the imperialists frankly acknowledged the primacy of self-interest and sought to turn an apparent vice into a virtue.

If the imperialist conception of national self-interest had been more in accord with traditional attitudes, Americans might have overlooked ethical incongruities; but time and public inertia absorbed the imperialist impulse, and self-interest reverted to its defensive posture. For a brief moment in history, when traditional self-interest was overwhelmed by a nationalistic urge for power and prestige, the proponents of expansion were able to capture the moral leadership of America; but when the aggressive conception of national self-interest subsided, imperialist idealism had to commend itself to the public on its own merits, and it suffered in the comparison of pretense with practice.

On the other hand, idealists, unlike egoists, were largely able to ignore the problem of reconciling national self-interest with missionary fervor, since they were in the enviable position of critics who did not have to test their own assumptions. They had no cause to doubt their major premise that, as long as the United States remained aloof from the political affairs of other nations, its self-interest would always be in perfect harmony with ideal principles. Whereas imperialists, unwilling to rely upon the Manifest Destiny they avowed, were actively engaged in the business of putting their ambitious conception of self-interest into practice, proponents of the status quo were inclined to take their view of self-interest for granted, in the comforting belief that America's prosperity and the progress of her institutions were as-

sured, almost automatically, by the nation's adherence to the alleged dicta of isolation set down for all time by the Forefathers.

The importance of this utopian assumption lies in the fact that it was, in large measure, common to all Americans. Many of the supporters of imperialism were as oblivious of the necessity of reconciling ideals with self-interest as the anti-imperialists. They were merely more naïve and less candid than Roosevelt, Mahan, and Lodge, and more insensitive to the demands of conscience than were the anti-imperialists. Few who embraced expansionism as a kind of nationalistic orgy comprehended the practical results of their ambition. In general, ultranationalists were no more burdened than the extreme idealists with the facts of world politics as they impinged upon American security. America's egoistic and altruistic impulses were equally free of a sense of the limitations prescribed by the realities of world politics. Accordingly, national self-assertiveness and national idealism displayed the same propensity for extravagance; and one impulse was as fickle as the other.

On the whole, America's first crusade gave little evidence of that steadiness of national purpose one associates with the mature possession of world power. On the eve of the war with Spain Richard Olney had warned that an irresponsible idealism threatened not only to render Americans contemptible in the eyes of the world, as a "nation of sympathizers and sermonizers and swaggers," but also to involve the United States in situations that would be positively detrimental to its self-interest; and he had pleaded that American idealism be tempered with a realistic appraisal of the nation's position in world politics. Whether or not his warning was premature would depend, to a large extent, upon circumstances beyond American control, but by the turn of the century his assessment of the

American approach to international relations seemed only too accurate; for although the nation had tasted the first fruits of world power, most Americans lingered in the age of innocence, naïve and scornful witnesses of the unsentimental calculation of national advantage which preoccupied the minds of military men and power-conscious statesmen and scholars.

Aware of the racism inherent in the thinking of many imperialists, historians have often assumed that anti-imperialists held opposite views. Accordingly, the debate between anti-imperialists and imperialists has usually been portrayed as one of liberals versus reactionaries, idealists versus materialists. CHRISTOPHER LASCH (1932-   ), a professor of history at Northwestern University, questions this characterization by demonstrating that the two antagonists had much more in common than is usually assumed. Lasch's essay is particularly useful in demonstrating how regional and parochial domestic considerations became intricately involved in the nation's expansionist policies. The essay also demonstrates that the imperialists and anti-imperialists were quite diverse jn their social and ideological make-up. °

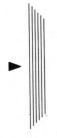

The Anti-imperialists and the Inequality of Man

The cession of the Philippine Islands to the United States precipitated a great debate on the nature of our foreign policy and our national destiny. Opinion on the wisdom of retaining the Philippines was divided without regard to party or section; indeed, the intrusion of the expansionist issue into the politics of the period tended for a time to obliterate sectionalism. Yet sectional considerations, particularly in the South, were not absent from the debate. Southern Democrats were almost unanimous in condemning "imperialism," on the grounds that Asiatics, like Negroes, were innately inferior to white people and could not be assimilated to American life. Two decades earlier such arguments would have called forth angry rejoinders from the

North. That the South's recourse to them at the end of the century did not revive the old controversy over Reconstruction revealed the extent to which Northern liberals had retreated from the implications of their emancipation of the Negro—a retreat the irony of which Southern statesmen never tired of expounding. An examination of the debate over imperialism helps to explain this remarkable change in Northern opinion and thereby enables us to see Southern racialism, so prevalent in the nineties, in a larger perspective. Thus a revaluation of an experience essentially national, not sectional, compels a revaluation of sectional history as well. Just as the corruption of the Reconstruction governments was paralleled by corruption in Northern state

°Christopher Lasch, "The Anti-Imperialists, the Philippines, and the Inequality of Man," *Journal of Southern History*, XIV (August, 1958), 319-331. Footnotes omitted.

governments and in Washington, as historians are beginning to show, so at a somewhat later date illiberalism in the South also had its counterpart in the North. The retreat from idealism was a national, not a local, phenomenon.

That Northerners of the expansionist persuasion made no reply to those who in the course of challenging the annexation of the Philippines challenged some of the fundamental assumptions of American democracy should come as no surprise. The expansionists were in a delicate predicament. Men who favored acquiring the Philippines on the grounds that the natives were unfit for self-government could hardly afford to apply another logic to the Negro problem in the South; Senator Henry Cabot Lodge, among others, might well look back on his recent Force Bill as a youthful indiscretion which it were prudent to forget. But one would not have expected anti-imperialists in the North to share this reluctance to revive the dispute over equality. Because they professed a fervid devotion to the rights of man, the anti-imperialists might have been expected to guide the debate over annexation to higher ground by rejecting outright the leading argument both of the expansionists and of the Southern anti-expansionists, namely that men are created unequal. Most historians have in fact assumed that anti-imperialism was genuinely liberal in inspiration and that the anti-imperialists were voicing objections to colonialism now commonly accepted.

The position of the anti-imperialists does at first appear to have been sensible and straightforward: that is, that imperialism was not only inexpedient but unjust, a departure from the historic principles of the Declaration of Independence. But a closer examination of certain facets of anti-imperialism may require us to see the anti-imperialists in a rather different light. Their

argument did not foreshadow the liberalism of the Good Neighbor policy. It was in fact no more liberal than that of the expansionists. Indeed, it resembled the expansionist rationale, against which it appeared to be a protest, far more closely than it does any of the objections we might today raise against a colonial policy, or for that matter than it resembled the theories of Thomas Jefferson. It was a product of the late nineteenth century, not of the eighteenth or twentieth centuries. The anti-imperialists, like the imperialists, saw the world from a pseudo-Darwinian point of view. They accepted the inequality of man—or, to be more precise, of races—as an established fact of life. They did not question the idea that Anglo-Saxons were superior to other people, and some of them would even have agreed that they were destined eventually to conquer the world. They did not quarrel with the idea of "destiny"; they merely refused to believe that destiny required such strenuous exertions of the American people, particularly when they saw in those exertions the menace of militarism and tyranny. There were important differences of opinion, of course, between those who favored and those who opposed the annexation of the Philippines, but for the moment it is perhaps more important to dwell on the matters on which they agreed. Most middle-class Americans of the 1890's agreed in attaching great importance to the concept of race, and it was that agreement which gave the intellectual life of the period its peculiar tone.

It is characteristic of the period that neither side in the debate over the Philippines was content to rest its case on considerations of expediency alone, although the expansionist clique on whom defense of the "large policy" devolved tried to rouse the business community, which was apathetic toward the whole question of expansion, with visions of glittering markets in China. But economic arguments could too easily be attacked as sordid, and the expansionists preferred to stand on higher ground. They appealed to "manifest destiny," an old idea, and to the newer, post-Darwinian idea that it was the manifest *duty* of higher civilizations to displace lower ones, either through outright elimination (as the white man had eliminated the Indian) or through a process of uplift and "Christianization." It was as carriers of civilization, they argued, that the American people were obliged to annex the Philippines, however disagreeable the obligation might appear.

The anti-imperialists, largely ignoring the economic and strategic arguments for annexation, replied with a moral argument of their own. They admitted that our history, as the expansionists were fond of showing, was a record of territorial expansion, but they fixed the limits of our westward destiny at the shores of the Pacific. The American destiny, they contended, was merely continental, not global. All of the areas previously acquired by the United States had been on the North American continent, and all except Alaska had been contiguous to the old states. Because they were contiguous and because they were thinly populated, they came to be settled by citizens from the older states, by white, Protestant, English-speaking people—by a population, in short, indistinguishable from that of the older states. The new territories, therefore, could be, and were, admitted to statehood. (Alaska, again, was the single exception.)

But to annex distant islands already heavily populated by racial aliens, the anti-imperialists maintained, would be a momentous and disastrous departure from the past. The Filipinos, for any number of reasons, could not become American citizens; they would have to be governed as subjects. But how could a republic have subjects?

For the United States to acquire the Philippines without admitting their people to full citizenship would amount to government without the consent of the governed—a flat contradiction of the cardinal principle of American democracy, the principle over which we separated from England, the principle of the Declaration of Independence. Nor was this all. As a result of the initial injustice, others would follow. A large standing army would have to be created in order to defend our new possessions not only against foreign powers but against the natives themselves, who were already in revolt against American rule; and an army called into being for the purpose of crushing freedom abroad would ultimately be used to destroy it at home. The administration had already begun to censor news from the Philippines, in order to create the impression that the hostilities there were purely defensive in character, and the anti-imperialists saw in this an evil omen—proof that if the United States persisted in imperialism, she would eventually go the way of Rome.

The exponents of annexation could offer no satisfactory answer to all this. Instead, they attempted to create a dilemma of their own—to show that there was no satisfactory alternative to annnexation. Accordingly they argued that the Filipinos were not "ready" for self-government and if left to themselves would fall into the hands of a native dictator or a foreign conqueror. But not a single expansionist proposed that the privileges of citizenship be extended to the Philippines. They assumed that the Filipinos would have to be governed as second-class citizens, and with that assumption they departed from the natural-rights philosophy of the Declaration of Independence, exactly as their antagonists accused them of doing. Senator Henry M. Teller, an expansionist, confessed that to hold the islanders as subjects would be "rather objec-

tionable in a republic"; but there seemed
no choice. Not all the expansionists had
similar reservations, but almost all of them
recognized and admitted the implications
of their policy for the doctrine of natural
rights. In effect, they substituted for the
Jeffersonian proposition that the right to
liberty is "natural"—hence universal—the
proposition that rights depend on
environment—on "civilization," of which
there were now seen to be many stages of
development; on race; even on climate. A
pseudo-Darwinian hierarchy of cultural
stages, unequal in the capacity for en-
joyment of the rights associated with self-
government, replaced the simpler and
more liberal theory of the Enlightenment,
which recognized only the distinction
between society and nature. "Rights," as
absolutes, lost their meaning by becoming
relative to time and place. Rights now depended on a people's "readiness" to enjoy
them.

It is not surprising that the anti-imperialists accused the expansionists of abandoning the Declaration of Independence.
What is surprising is that their own arguments were no closer to the spirit of that
document than the ones they denounced
with such fervor. The anti-imperialists were
in fact no more Jeffersonian in their essential outlook than Theodore Roosevelt or
Henry Cabot Lodge or Alfred T. Mahan
was, for they did not challenge the central
assumption of imperialist thought: the natural inequality of men. The imperialists at
least had the merit of consistency; they
made no professions of Jeffersonianism.
The anti-imperialists, on the other hand,
invoked the name of Jefferson at every opportunity.

Some light on the anti-imperialists is
shed by the high proportion of Southerners
among them. In the Senate, only four of
twenty-eight Southern senators favored
unconditional ratification of the treaty with

Spain, and Southerners led the attack on
the treaty in debate. Their arguments
against ratification clearly reflected the lin-
gering bitterness of Reconstruction, as well
as more recent movements to exclude
Negroes from the benefits of citizenship.
Annexation of the Philippines, they argued,
would merely compound the race problem
by introducing into the country what Senator John W. Daniel of Virginia called a
"mess of Asiatic pottage." Benjamin R.
Tillman of South Carolina was especially
active in the anti-imperialist cause, playing
ingenious variations on the racial theme. At
times he gave it a distinctly Darwinian
note: ". . .we [he said, referring to the
South] understand and realize what it is to
have two races side by side that can not mix
or mingle without deterioration and injury
to both and the ultimate destruction of the
civilization of the higher." At other times
he gave it a pro-labor bias: ". . .here are
10,000,000 Asiatics who will have the right
as soon as the pending treaty is ratified, to
get on the first ship that they can reach and
come here and compete in the labor market
of the United States." In a more somber
mood, he appeared to speak more in sorrow
than in anger: ". . .coming. . .as a Senator
from. . .South Carolina, with 750,000 colored population and only 500,000 whites, I
realize what you are doing, while you don't;
and I would save this country from the in-
jection into it of another race question
which can only breed bloodshed and a
costly war and the loss of the lives of our
brave soldiers." More often, however, he
spoke with biting irony which revealed the
Negro, not the Filipino, as the real source of
his anxiety and, further, which showed that
he was more interested in embarrassing the
North—in forcing its senators to admit to a
contradiction—than he was in preventing
the acquisition of the Philippines. When
Knute Nelson of Minnesota, once an aboli-
tionist, declared that the Filipinos were in-

capable of self-government, Tillman replied: "I want to call the Senator's attention to the fact, however, that he and others who are now contending for a different policy in Hawaii and the Philippines gave the slaves of the South not only self-government, but they forced on the white men of the South, at the point of the bayonet, the rule and domination of those ex-slaves. Why the difference? Why the change? Do you acknowledge that you were wrong in 1868?"

It is unnecessary to insist that such arguments did not spring from a deep-seated attachment to the Declaration of Independence. But it would be manifestly unfair to judge the whole anti-imperialist movement on the basis of its Southern wing, particularly when many Northern men of the persuasion were clearly uncomfortable at finding themselves in the company of men like Tillman. An examination of their own arguments, however, discloses no important difference from that of the Southerners, except that Northern anti-imperialists did not dwell on the parallel with the Southern Negro problem—something they were by this time anxious to forget. One is left with the impression that it was not the Southern argument as such that disconcerted the Northerners, but the use to which the South put it. When it came to giving reasons why the Philippines should not be annexed, North and South found themselves in close agreement.

Anti-imperialists contended that the Filipinos, unless they were given their independence, would have to be held in subjection, since they could not be admitted as citizens. What is interesting is the manner in which they arrived at the latter conclusion. A brief study of the process reveals a Darwinism as thoroughgoing as that of the imperialists themselves.

In the first place, the anti-imperialists argued, if the Filipinos became citizens, they would migrate to the United States and compete with American labor—a prospect especially alarming in view of the racial composition of the islands. As Samuel Gompers declared: "If the Philippines are annexed, what is to prevent the Chinese, the Negritos, and the Malays coming to our own country?" This was more than an economic argument. It implied that those people were accustomed to a low standard of living and, what is more, that they were incapable, by virtue of their race, of longing for anything better. It implied that Orientals, in short, would work for low wages because they could not, and never would, appreciate the finer things of life which money alone could buy. This view had already come into vogue on the West Coast, where it was particularly popular with organized labor; it is not surprising, therefore, to find Gompers appealing to it.

If cheap Filipino labor would compete unfairly with American labor, cheap Filipino goods could be expected to compete unfairly with American goods. If we took over the islands, we could neither prevent immigration nor levy protective import duties. Annexation would therefore injure both capital and labor.

But the Filipinos would also be given the vote. Considering, again, the racial composition of the islands, the results would clearly be ruinous. Carl Schurz declared:

If they become states on an equal footing with the other states they will not only be permitted to govern themselves as to their home concerns, but will take part in governing the whole republic, in governing us, by sending senators and representatives into our Congress to help make our laws, and by voting for president and vice-president to give our national government its executive. The prospect of the consequences which would follow the admission of the Spanish creoles and the negroes of the West India islands and of the Malays and Tagals of the Philippines to participation in the conduct of our government is so alarming that you instinctively pause before taking the step.

The same sentiments were expressed by James L. Blair of St. Louis, the son of the old Free Soil leader Francis Preston Blair. "History," Blair said, "shows no instance of a tropical people who have demonstrated a capacity for maintaining an enduring form of Republican government." To admit such a people into a share in the government of the United States would be self-destructive. David Starr Jordan warned his countrymen: "If we govern the Philippines, so in their degree must the Philippines govern us. Or as Champ Clark put it even more forcefully in the House of Representatives: "No matter whether they are fit to govern themselves or not, they are not fit to govern us [applause]."

But if it was undesirable for the Filipinos to come to the United States or to take part in American government, was it not still possible that Americans would emigrate to the Philippines and gradually displace the native culture? The anti-imperialists denied that any such outcome was possible. In the first place, "the two races could never amalgamate"; "the racial differences between the Oriental and Western races are never to be eradicated." But suppose the Filipinos were eliminated by force or herded into reservations, like the American Indians. Even then, the anti-imperialists insisted, annexation would be unwise, for the fact was that neither the "northern" (or "Anglo-Saxon" or "Germanic") race nor democratic institutions could survive in a tropical climate. "Civilization," said Jordan, "is, as it were, suffocated in the tropics." On another occasion he explained that the Philippines "lie in the heart of the torrid zone, 'Nature's asylum for degenerates.' " "Neither the people nor the institutions of the United States can ever occupy the Philippines," he said. "The

American home cannot endure there, the town-meeting cannot exist." Schurz echoed the same refrain:

They are. . .situated in the tropics, where people of the northern races, such as Anglo-Saxons, or generally speaking, people of Germanic blood, have never migrated in mass to stay; and they are more of less densely populated, parts of them as densely as Massachusetts—their population consisting almost exclusively of races to whom the tropical climate is congenial—. . . Malays, Tagals, Filipinos, Chinese, Japanese, Negritos, and various more or less barbarous tribes. . . .

Such arguments clearly showed that the anti-imperialists had abandoned the natural-rights philosophy of the Declaration of Independence for a complicated Darwinian view of the world. According to this view, which appeared to be substantiated by the science of the day and by the writings of historians like Herbert Baxter Adams, geography, race, and political institutions were inextricably intertwined. The temperate zone—specifically the northern part of it—bred the "Germanic" race, from which Americans were descended. Free institutions were associated with the rise of that race; a study of other cultures showed no similar institutions. Because they alone were capable of using liberty wisely, the Germans had already risen to a cultural level far beyond that of any other race and were possibly destined to supplant all others. In view of their inability to survive in the tropics, however, it was not quite clear how this was to be accomplished; and for that reason, perhaps, the anti-imperialists preferred to see the Anglo-Saxons stay at home, in their native habitat. In any case, to mingle their blood with that of Asiatics would be a fatal departure from what Charles Francis Adams, for example, called the "cardinal principle in our policy as a race." He referred to our Indian policy, which he admitted had been harsh; but it had "saved the Anglo-Saxon stock from being a nation of half-breeds." The acquisition of the Philippines would again endanger the purity of the old stock, on which America's very survival depended.

An examination of the arguments against annexation of the Philippines leads to a number of interesting conclusions. In the first place, it is difficult, after having read their writings and speeches, to convince oneself that the anti-imperialist had the better of the argument, as historians have tended to assume. Whatever the merits of the expansionists' contention that the Filipinos were not ready for self-government, the expansionists were at least consistent in the conclusions which they drew from it. If it was true that the Filipinos could not govern themselves, the humane policy (although not necessarily the wisest one) was to govern them ourselves. The anti-imperialists, on the other hand, while sharing the expansionists' basic assumption (an assumption contrary to the spirit of American democracy), were perfectly willing to leave the Filipinos to their fate—certainly a most un-Christian policy if they were indeed unable to manage their own affairs. So far as the moral argument had any validity at all, the anti-imperialists were on weak ground; and since they insisted on treating the question as a matter of right and wrong, it seems fair to judge them accordingly.

But it is not possible to condemn anti-imperialists for holding certain opinions on race unless one is willing to condemn the entire society of which they were a part. The fact is that the atmosphere of the late nineteenth century was so thoroughly permeated with racist thought (reinforced by Darwinism) that few men managed to escape it. The idea that certain cultures and races were naturally inferior to others was almost universally held by educated, middle-class, respectable Americans—in other words, by the dominant majority. The widespread and almost unconscious adherence to it was unmistakably manifested, in the same period, in the national policy toward minorities more familiar to American experience than the Filipinos, and in particular toward immigrants and Negroes. This was the period of the first serious restrictions on immigration; it was the period of the South's successful re-elimination of the Negro from white society. Men who called themselves liberals—survivors of the antislavery crusade and the battles of the sixties and seventies on behalf of the Negroes: liberal Republicans, mugwumps, "independents"—acquiesced in these developments. A study of anti-imperialism makes it a little clearer why they did, for the anti-imperialist movement was dominated by these same men—men like Schurz, Adams, Jordan, and Moorfield Storey. Except for Storey, these men had now receded from their earlier idealism. They continued to speak of their part in the struggle for Negro rights, to refer to it with pride, but by referring to it as a fight which had already been won they indicated their indifference to the continuing plight of the Southern Negro. Indeed, they had abandoned him, as they now proposed to abandon the Filipinos. They had no further interest in crusading; the times, it appeared, called for retrenchment.

Like Walter LaFeber, WILLIAM A. WILLIAMS (1921-   ), diplomatic and intellectual historian at the University of Wisconsin, sees the search for foreign markets as a major force shaping American expansion. Similarly, he sees much more rationality and calculation in the government's policy making than do Hofstadter and Halle. And like Lasch, Williams tends to stress the common outlook of imperialists and anti-imperialists. He suggests that the Open Door policy provided the opportunity for economic expansion without the expense of maintaining an empire. Moreover, the policy provided the means for settling the conflict between the imperialists and anti-imperialists. But was the Open Door policy deliberately chosen as a means for compromising the differences between the imperialists and anti-imperialists, or was the settlement of the differences an effect of the policy for which the McKinley Administration had not consciously planned?*

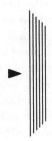

► ## *Imperial Anticolonialism*

Important to an understanding of twentieth-century American diplomacy is the manner in which the underlying bipartisan agreement on overseas economic expansion resolved the debate over whether or not America should embark upon a program of colonialism. Beginning with Admiral George Dewey's victory at Manila Bay and ending shortly after the election of 1900 (if not sooner), the argument is usually interpreted as a battle between the imperialists led by Theodore Roosevelt and the anti-imperialists led by William Jennings Bryan. It is more illuminating, however, to view it as a three-cornered discussion won by businessmen and intellectuals who opposed traditional colonialism and advocated instead the policy of an open door for America's overseas economic expansion.

Discounted in recent years as a futile and naive gesture in a world of harsh reality, the Open Door Policy was in fact a brilliant strategic stroke which led to the gradual extension of American economic and political power throughout the world. If it ultimately failed, it was not because it was foolish or weak, but because it was so successful. The empire that was built according to the strategy and tactics of the Open Door Notes engendered the antagonisms created by all empires, and it is that opposition which has posed so many difficulties for American diplomacy in the middle of the twentieth century.

*Reprinted from William A. Williams, *The Tragedy of American Diplomacy* (The World Publishing Company, 1959), pp. 34-40. Copyright© 1959 by William Appleman Williams. Reprinted by permission of the publisher.

At the outset, it is true, the debate between imperialists and anti-imperialists revolved around an actual issue—colonialism. Touched off by the specific question of what to do with Cuba and the Philippines, the battle raged over whether they should be kept as traditional colonies or established as quasi-independent nations under the benevolent supervision of the United States. Though the differences were significant at the beginning of the argument, it is nevertheless clear that they were never absolute. The Open Door Notes took the fury out of the fight. And within five years the issue was almost nonexistent. The anti-imperialists who missed that changing nature of the discussion were ultimately shocked and disillusioned when Bryan became Secretary of State and began to practice what they thought he condemned.

Such critics were mistaken in attacking Bryan as a backslider or a hypocrite. Bryan's foreign policy was not classical colonialism, but neither was it anti-imperial. He had never shirked his share of the white man's burden, though perhaps he did shoulder a bit more of the ideological baggage than the economic luggage. He was as eager for overseas markets as any but the most extreme agrarian and industrial expansionists. As with most other farmers, labor leaders, and businessmen, economic logic accounts for much of Bryan's anticolonialism. Looking anxiously for markets abroad as a way of improving conditions at home, all such men feared and opposed the competition of native labor. It was that consideration, as much as racism and Christian fundamentalism, that prompted Bryan to assert that "the Filipinos cannot be citizens without endangering our civilization."

Bryan's program for the Philippines symbolizes the kind of imperial anticolonialism that he advocated. Once the Philippine insurrection was crushed, he proposed that the United States should establish "a stable form of government" in the islands and then "protect the Philippines from outside interference while they work out their destiny, just as we have protected the republics of Central and South America, and are, by the Monroe Doctrine, pledged to protect Cuba." Opposition spokesmen gleefully pointed out that this was the substance of their own program.

Bryan also supported the kind of expansion favored by such Democrats as ex-President Grover Cleveland and ex-Secretary of State Richard Olney. "The best thing of the kind I have ever heard," remarked Cleveland of Olney's famous assertion that the United States "is practically sovereign on this continent, and its fiat is law upon the subjects to which it confines its interposition." As for Hawaii, Cleveland (and Bryan) wanted to control "the ports of a country so near to Japan and China" without the bother and responsibilites of formal annexation. Informal empire is perhaps the most accurate description of such a program. Both Cleveland and Bryan favored the overseas expansion of the American economic system and the extension of American authority throughout the world.

So, too, did such men as Roosevelt, Hay, and Lodge. At first, however, they stressed the acquisition of colonies, if not in the traditional sense of colonialism, at least in the pattern of administrative colonialism developed by Great Britain after the Indian Mutiny of 1857. Thus the early arguments between Roosevelt and Bryan were to some point. But the Roosevelt imperialists rather quickly modified their position in line with the argument advanced by such men as Brooks Adams. None of these leaders were motivated by a personal economic motive, but by concentrating on the economic issue, other more important considerations were overlooked. The Roosevelt group defined their economic interest in terms of preventing the stagnation of the American economic system, and their program to accomplish that objective was vigorous overseas economic expansion.

Following the thesis developed by Adams, they argued that the American system had to expand or stagnate. Businessmen agreed, interpreting that general economic analysis in terms of their specific and immediate economic motive for more markets. Imperialism or no imperialism, the nation agreed, our trade must be protected. But defined in that fashion, trade was no longer the exchange of commodities and services between independent producers meeting in the market place; it became instead a euphemism for the control of foreign markets for America's industrial and agricultural surpluses.

Secretary of State John Hay's Open Door Notes of 1899 and 1900 distilled this collection of motivations, pressures, and theories into a classic program of imperial expansion. Based on the assumption of what Brooks Adams called "America's economic supremacy," and formulated in the context of vigorous pressure from domestic economic interests and the threatening maneuvers of other nations, the policy of the open door was designed to establish the conditions under which America's preponderant economic power would extend the American system throughout the world without the embarrassment and inefficiency of traditional colonialism. Hay's first note of 1899 asserted the right of access for American economic power into China in particular, but the principle was rapidly generalized to the rest of the world. His second note of 1900 was designed to prevent other nations from extending the formal colonial system to China, and in later years that also was applied to other areas.

The Open Door Notes ended the debate between imperialists and anti-imperialists. The argument trailed on with the inertia characteristic of all such disagreements, but the nation recognized and accepted Hay's policy as a resolution of the original issue. In a similar fashion, it took some years (and further discussion) to liquidate the colonial status of the territory seized during the Spanish-American War. It also required time to work out and institutionalize a division of authority and labor between economic and political leaders so that the strategy could be put into operation on a routine basis. And it ultimately became necessary to open the door into existing colonial empires as well as unclaimed territories. But Secretary of State Hay's policy of the open door synthesized and formalized the frontier thesis, the specific demands of businessmen, workers, and farmers, and the theory which asserted that the American economic system would stagnate if it did not expand overseas.

America and the world shared this interpretation of the Open Door Policy at the time it was enunciated. Brooks Adams eulogized Secretary Hay as the realist who industrialized the Monroe Doctrine. The Philadelphia *Press* agreed: "This new doctrine established for China is destined to be as important as the Monroe Doctrine has been for the Americas in the past century. It protects the present, it safeguards the future." Quite aware of the. grand design, the Boston *Transcript* spelled it out in blunt accents. "We have an infinitely wider scope in the Chinese markets than we should have had with a 'sphere of influence' in competition with half a dozen other spheres." Many European commentators acknowledged that the strategy "hits us in our weak spot." Agreeing with the Boston analysis, a Berlin paper summed it up in one sentence: "The Americans regard, in a certain sense, all China as their sphere of interest."

Ex-Secretary of State Olney made it bipartisan. Prepared for the Presidential election campaign of 1900, in which he supported Bryan, Olney's statement of the new imperial consensus was at the same time an excellent review of America's new foreign policy. "The 'home market' fallacy disappears," he explained, 'with the proved inadequacy of the home market. Nothing will satisfy us in the future but free access to foreign markets—especially to those markets in the East." As one convinced at an early date by Brooks Adams that noncolonial economic expansion was the best strategy, Olney regretted the acquisition of the Philippines. It would have been wiser to have followed Washington's advice of 1796 and the principles of the Monroe Doctrine. "The true, the ideal position for us," Olney explained, "would be complete freedom of action, perfect liberty to pick allies from time to time as special occasions might warrant and an enlightened view of our own interests might dictate." But he was confident that the policy of the open door provided the very best approximation to that ideal.

Americans of that era and their European competitors were basically correct in their estimate of the Open Door Policy. It was neither an alien idea foisted off on America by the British nor a political gesture to the domestic crowd. Latter-day experts who dismissed the policy as irrelevant, misguided, or unsuccessful erred in two respects. They missed its deep roots in the American past and its importance at the time, and they failed to realize that the policy expressed the basic strategy and tactics of America's secular and imperial expansion in the twentieth century. When combined with the ideology of an industrial Manifest Destiny, the history of the Open Door Notes became the history of American foreign relations from 1900 to 1958.

While certain principles of the Open Door policy were part of a long tradition in American diplomacy, the policy was fashioned in response to the plans of various European powers to divide China into spheres of influence. As historians have long debated over why the McKinley Administration acted by sending the Open Door notes, CHARLES S. CAMPBELL, JR. (1911-   ), a professor of history at Claremont Graduate School, undertook the following case study in order to demonstrate the role that specific interest groups played in shaping the policy. By relating the Open Door policy to the McKinley Administration's interest in promoting American economic expansionism abroad, Campbell's interpretation of the policy is much closer to that of Williams than to the explanations offered by George F. Kennan (pp. 109-117).°

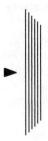

The Role of Business Interests

One of the basic aims of American foreign policy has been to maintain the right of all countries to trade with China on an equal basis. The first formal declaration of this aim came with the sending of the Open Door notes in September, 1899. The origin of these notes has received much attention from historians in recent years, and certain aspects of their origin, particularly the part played by W. W. Rockhill and the Englishman, Alfred Hippisley, have become very well known. At least one aspect, however, has been entirely overlooked: namely, that special business interests in the United States were concerned over the possible loss of the Chinese market; were eager to have the government take just the sort of action which it did take;

and were active in bringing pressure to bear on the government. It is the thesis of this article that they were partly responsible for the sending of the notes and, consequently, for America's Open Door policy.

It should be emphatically stated, however, that this article does not pretend to give a complete account of the Open Door policy. Not only does the author not believe that such an account can be given merely in terms of business pressure on Washington, but the article does not even consider business in general; it is limited almost exclusively to two groups of special interests, which might, indeed, be called one, so closely did they overlap. The almost complete absence of reference to many of the well-known aspects of the origin of the

°Charles S. Campbell, Jr. "American Business Interests and the Open Door," *The Far Eastern Quarterly*, I (1949), 43-58. Reprinted by permission of The Journal of Asian Studies. Footnotes omitted.

policy does not mean that the author considers these factors unimportant, but simply that he is confining himself to what has not been elaborated elsewhere. Numerous writers have attempted to give a rounded account of the matter; a very few have gone deeply into the part played by business; but no writer has dealt specifically with the special interests here under consideration. Yet the influence of these interests appears to have been so great that any complete history of the origins of the Open Door policy should include some mention of them.

One of these special interests was the American-China Development Company, a corporation founded in 1895 for the purpose of getting railroad concessions in China. Its sixty shares of stock were held by forty-nine shareholders, of whom the best known were the following: the Carnegie Steel Company; Thomas C. Platt, Senator from New York; Levi P. Morton, vice-president of the United States under President Harrison; Frederick P. Olcott, president of the Central Trust Company of New York; John I. Waterbury, president of the Manhattan Trust Company; James Stillman, president of the National City Bank; George F. Baker, president of the First National Bank of New York; Charles Coster, member of J. P. Morgan and Company; Jacob Schiff, member of Kuhn, Loeb, and Company; E. H. Harriman, chairman of the executive committee of the Union Pacific Railway; and G. R. Hegeman, president of the Metropolitan Life Insurance Company. Three officials of the Development Company were also important shareholders: A. W. Bash, its representative in China; General William Barclay Parsons, its chief engineer; and Clarence Cary, its legal adviser. With seven shares of stock, Cary was the company's chief shareholder.

Shortly after the formation of the Ameri-can-China Development Company, Bash was sent to China to try to get a concession. In May, 1895, he called on Charles Denby, the American minister in Peking, and asked for his assistance. Since Denby had for years been trying to persuade Americans to do business in China, he was anxious to do what he could for Bash; but in view of the State Department's traditional caution about supporting private business interests, he thought it prudent to ask for instructions from Washington.

About this time Richard Olney became Secretary of State. As an advocate of more vigorous support for American enterprise in foreign countries than most of his predecessors, it is not surprising to find him advising Denby "to employ all proper methods for the extension of American commercial interests." It was perhaps as a result of this note that Bash secured shortly afterwards a preliminary contract for a railway concession between Peking and Hankow. But Bash was not empowered to conclude the contract; it was, therefore, necessary to wait until authorized agents of the company should arrive in China. When the agents, one of whom was Clarence Cary, did arrive, they found the Chinese refusing to continue negotiations. Accordingly, they complained to Denby. The minister called on the Chinese foreign office and told the officials that it would be a "a breach of good faith" not to go through with the contract. Taking a strong line, he succeeded in persuading the Chinese to resume negotiations.

Meanwhile Olney had been succeeded by John Sherman, a man who did not believe in government support for such ventures as the Development Company. When the new Secretary of State read Denby's official report about the above incident, he was not pleased. "You should be cautious," he warned the minister, "in giving what might be understood as this Government's indorsement of the financial standing of the persons seeking contracts with that of China." It is not wholly surprising, therefore, that two months later a Belgian syndicate, instead of the American-China Development Company, was awarded the contract.

Despite the turn of events the Americans continued their efforts to obtain a concession somewhere in China; but the year closed with no success to report. Did the officials and the powerful shareholders of the Development Company know of Sherman's warning to Denby? Whether they did or not, they must have found little to their liking in the negative policy of the State Department under its new Secretary; and some of them took part in the organized attempt, as will be noted in what follows, to persuade the government to adopt a different policy.

A second group of special interests was the American exporters of cotton goods. Cotton goods were America's chief export to China, and that country provided by far the largest market for American cotton mills. In 1899 this country exported $24,852,691 worth of cotton goods, of which almost half, $10,290,981, went to China alone. No other country came close to this, the second largest importer taking only about one-fourth as much.

At that time England was the leading exporter of cotton goods to China, the United States was second, and far in the rear were Japan and the Netherlands. Although the annual value of the American exports was only about half that of the English, it had increased over 120 per cent from 1887 to 1897; while English exports had declined almost 14 per cent. Americans attached considerable importance to this rapid growth of exports. They believed that the United States was capturing the Chinese market and that it was a market well worth acquiring. Even those with little or no business in China were impressed, for

they had great hopes for the future. In those times, as still today, China was considered in wide circles to be potentially the greatest market in the world.

We have, then, in the case of cotton, an American industry vitally concerned with the Chinese market. As many members of the industry were almost altogether dependent on that market, anything which the government might do to preserve it would be their direct interest. The same, of course, was true of the American-China Development Company. The men connected with this company, along with the cotton exporters, were those who had the greatest financial interest in China, and it was they who were most active in bringing pressure to bear on the American government. Of course, business anxiety over the Chinese market was by no means limited to these two groups, but as they had so much more at stake than any other group, it would be misleading not to give them special treatment.

The first step taken by these special interests occurred at the beginning of 1898. At that time considerable anxiety arose out of developments in China. The previous March, France had made the island of Hainan a sphere of influence; in November, German troops had landed at Kiaochow; and shortly afterwards a Russian fleet had dropped anchor at Port Arthur. It looked to many businessmen as though something which they had been fearing for several years—the partition of China—might be on the verge of realization. The threat to Port Arthur was particularly disturbing to Americans, for it was a key city of Manchuria, which, together with the adjoining provinces of China proper, was the chief market for American cotton goods. It was widely expected that, should Russia get control, discriminatory tariffs would be introduced, and an important market would be lost to the United States.

Business opinion was also aroused by the

attitude of the State Department. Despite what seemed to be so obviously a dangerous situation in China, responsible officials were giving no sign of alarm; in fact, they seemed almost to welcome the situation. Interviewed by the Philadelphia *Press*, Secretary Sherman stated that he did not see any likelihood of partition—at least, not for some time. Even if China should be partitioned, he said, "the powers would gladly seize the opportunity to trade with us. Our commercial interests would not suffer, as far as I can see, in the least—quite the contrary."

This expression of opinion was most disturbing to those with financial interests in China. In an article which he wrote apparently just after Sherman's statement, Clarence Cary, back from his unsuccessful trip to China in behalf of the American-China Development Company, denounced what he termed the Secretary's "quaint and dangerous view that the interests of the citizens of the United States are not threatened by a possible partition of China." In a similar vein, the New York *Journal of Commerce and Commercial Bulletin*, a newspaper which often expressed the point of view of many cotton exporters, spoke in a strongly worded editorial of the "generally admitted necessity of prompting the Administration to give notice to the world that the United States will suffer no interference with the commercial rights it now possesses in China."

This combination of encroachment on Chinese soil and evidence of what they took to be disinterestedness on the part of the State Department so alarmed some of those with financial interests in China that they determined to take action. On January 6, 1898, three days after Sherman's statement to the *Press*, they held a meeting in the office of Clarence Cary in New York City. At the meeting a "Committee on American Interests in China" was founded. It was instructed to confer, first with the New York Chamber of Commerce, and then, if it should seem desirable, with other commercial organizations throughout the country, regarding "the methods to be adopted to conserve the rights of citizens of the United States in the Chinese Empire.". . .

Just a week after its founding the committee submitted to the New York Chamber of Commerce a petition signed by a large number of important firms. The petition urged the chamber to take such action as would direct the attention of the government to the threatening situation in China and would ensure "that the important commercial interests of the United States" be safeguarded. As a result of the petition the chamber adopted the following memorial on February 3 and forwarded it to President McKinley the same day:

That there are important changes now going on in the relations of European powers to the Empire of China. . .affecting the privileges enjoyed under existing treaty rights by American citizens trading in and with China. That the trade of the United States to China is now rapidly increasing, and is destined, with the further opening of that country, to assume large proportions unless arbitrarily debarred by the action of foreign governments. . . .That, in view of the changes threatening to future trade development of the United States in China, the Chamber of Commerce. . .respectfully and earnestly urge that such proper steps be taken as will commend themselves to your wisdom for the prompt and energetic defence of the existing treaty rights of our citizens in China, and for the preservation and protection of their important commercial interests in that Empire.

Secretary Sherman, to whom the President had referred the memorial, informed the New York Chamber that the matter was being given the "most careful consideration." As a matter of fact, the same day that he wrote to the chamber he instructed the ambassador in Berlin to inform the authorities in that country of "the interest which this Government must necessarily feel in conserving and expanding the volume of trade which it has built up with China." If, as seems probable, this step was in part the result of the above memorial, it was the first success of the special interests in influencing the policy of the government.

During the first four months of 1898 there were several further developments which originated in the Committee on American Interests in China. The committee had communicated with the commercial organizations of Philadelphia, Boston, San Francisco, and Cleveland, as well as with that of New York, and during this period all except the Cleveland Chamber sent to Washington memorials similar to the one quoted above. Not quite so directly attributable to the committee were memorials received by the government from the Chambers of Commerce of Baltimore and Seattle. That they were inspired, at least indirectly, by the Committee on American Interests is evident in the fact that they were almost identical in wording with the memorial from the New York Chamber. It might also be mentioned that a number of American businessmen in China sent a telegram to the New York body, endorsing its memorial and stating that "immediate action" was necessary for the protection of American interests. This message was forwarded to the State Department.

The adoption of these memorials of early 1898 is doubtless to be attributed not only to the Committee on American Interests but also to events taking place in China during these same months. In February, China was forced to promise Great Britain that the rich Yangtze provinces would never be alienated to another power. This came as something of a shock to Americans, for Britain was commonly regarded as one of the bulwarks of the Open Door in China.

Two months later a similar agreement regarding some of the southern provinces was made with France. Most alarming of all were the settlements with Germany and Russia in March—settlements which wound up the Kiaochow and Port Arthur affairs, the beginnings of which have been referred to. Germany succeeded in obtaining a ninety-nine-year lease of the land around Kiaochow Bay, along with extensive economic rights in Shantung province. Russia, after an acute crisis which almost led to war with Great Britain, secured a twenty-five-year lease of the southern tip of the Liaotung peninsula, with the right of building a railway to its principal city, Port Arthur. A more direct threat to the North China market could hardly have been imagined.

Despite both the ominous developments in the Far East and the memorials urging action, the State Department was not pursuing a forceful line. Apart from the mild warning to Germany mentioned above, the only positive step taken during the first part of 1898 was the sending of a telegram by the Secretary of State to Ambassador Hitchcock in St. Petersburg. Hitchcock was instructed to sound out Russia's intentions and to inform the Russian government that the United States was anxious to "maintain open trade in China." Although it was not at all the strong kind of move desired by the special interests, this *démarche* represented a further step in the evolution of the State Department away from the extreme indifference of Sherman earlier in the year. Together with the telegram to Germany it suggests that the memorials originating in the Committee on American Interests were having some effect in Washington.

Not only the government, but also the public in general, was becoming more conscious of the China market; and here too, part of the change must be attributed to the Committee on American Interests in

China. Since the memorials inspired by it had been widely discussed in the press, they had reached a larger audience than government circles, and they had not been without effect on public opinion. . . .

The war with Spain. which began in April, 1898, brought with it a rising tide of imperialistic sentiment in the United States. Caught up in this tide and modified by it was the American attitude toward the complex situation in China. To be sure, there was no widespread thought of China as a possible colony, or even of a sphere-of-influence there, but, as Professor Pratt has shown, the foothold which the triumph at Manila Bay gave us in the Philippines was considered by many to be important chiefly because it might help us to hold open the door in the Far East. Then too the fact that America seemed to be suddenly growing up into a great power probably had the effect of making Americans more insistent that treaty rights, including those in China, be upheld.

During the war one of the most important developments in the history of the origins of the Open Door policy took place. The Committee on American Interests had come to the decision that a more permanent form of organization was needed, and to meet that need the committee was transformed in June, 1898, into the American Asiatic Association. The association had the same general aim as its predecessor. As stated in its constitution, this was "to secure the advantage of sustained watchfulness and readiness for action. . .in respect of. . .Asiatic trade, as well as in matters of legislation, or treaties affecting the same.". . .

The American Asiatic Association was the principal channel through which the special interests made their influence felt in Washington and in the country at large. It was strongly supported by the *Journal of Commerce and Commercial Bulletin*, which devoted an extraordinary amount of editorial and news space to questions of the Chinese market and consistently advocated energetic action by the government to safeguard that market. Co-operation between the association and the journal was doubtless facilitated by the fact that John Foord occupied an important position in each of these guardians of American interests in the Far East.

The founding of the Asiatic Association was the chief event concerned with the origins of the Open Door policy which took place during the war with Spain. However, a few other developments of the same time, though of comparatively minor importance, may also be mentioned.

Perhaps the outstanding of these was a recommendation to Congress by Sherman's successor in the State Department, William R. Day, that a trade commission be sent to China to investigate possibilities for greater exports to that part of the world. Although Congress took no action at the time, the incident has some significance as marking a further step in the evolution of the government toward the point of view of the special interests.

Also of significance was the appointment of John Hay to the position of Secretary of State. In view of the memorials of the early part of the year and such a further indication of the opinion of influential businessmen as the establishment of the Asiatic Association, it is quite possible that Hay's well-known propensity for the Open Door in China was one of the reasons for his appointment. Hardly had he assumed office when the new Secretary showed that his Far Eastern policy was going to be stronger than that of his two predecessors. Perhaps as a result of a memorial from one of the American establishments in China, stating that there was a "probability of serious interference [by Russia] with America's important trade in cotton. . .unless immediate steps are taken in Peking to insist that our treaty rights with China be maintained." Hay ordered two gunboats to proceed to North China. The New York Chamber of Commerce, incidentally, expressed its "high appreciation" of the act. For the time being, however, nothing further came of the Russian threat.

The last event we need mention which occurred during the war was the annual message to Congress of President McKinley. Repeating Day's recommendation of a trade commission, the President stated that the United States was not an "indifferent spectator" of what was going on in China but that it would preserve its "large interests in that quarter by all means appropriate to the constant policy of our Government." This strong declaration was naturally hailed with delight by those with business interests in China.

When the war with Spain formally came to an end early in 1899 with the ratification of the peace treaty by the Senate, the government was able to turn its attention from military matters to such peacetime consideration as trade with China. In January it received an important memorial. Coming from a large number of cotton manufacturers, the memorial stated that the Chinese market would be lost to American cotton exporters "unless a vigorous policy is pursued on the part of the . . .Government"; it requested that the American diplomatic representatives at Peking and St. Petersburg "be instructed to give special attention to the subject." This memorial seems to have impressed Secretary Hay even more than the memorial of the preceding January had impressed Sherman. Referring to the "high character and standing of the signers," he ordered the envoys to give the "special attention" requested of them; and about a month later, apparently afraid he had not been sufficiently emphatic, he wrote a second time to the ambassador to Russia, asking him to continue "to act energetically in the sense desired by the numerous and influential signers of the petition."

Another episode of early 1899 worth mentioning was the Asiatic Association's strong support of a protest by the United States against an attempt by France to extend her concession in Shanghai. The association wrote to McKinley and Hay, urging that "all available means" be used "towards preserving for the world's commerce an 'open door' in the Far East." In sharp contrast with this was the association's viewpoint regarding an attempt to obtain an extension of the combined British and American concession. Negotiations with China had been going on for some time but without success. Angered and alarmed, the association informed Secretary Hay of "the necessity of. . .vigorous action. . .in order to obtain a definite solution." Sending a copy of this letter to the minister to China, Hay instructed him to devote his efforts to obtaining the extension. Two months later China gave way.

In March the campaign for the Open Door took a more decisive turn. It became known at that time that Italy was endeavoring to secure from the Chinese government a lease of Sanmen Bay, a bay located not far from Shanghai, the center of foreign business in China. Fears of partition once again rose quickly to the surface. There was widespread suspicion that Italy had the backing of Great Britain; if true, it would mean that the only remaining great power opposed to the partition of China was the United States.

The situation disturbed the American Asiatic Association to an extent which might seem surprising today. Today we know that the Sanmen Bay affair turned out to be a comparatively insignificant incident. But to those who lived at the time of the crisis itself this knowledge was lacking, and to them, fearful as they were that it would take very little indeed to start off the process of dismembering China, the spring of 1899 was a time of grave anxiety. So disturbing was the situation to the officials of the Asiatic Association that they held a series of meetings in order to discuss the possibility of a fundamental modification of the policy they had been pursuing.

As has been shown, this policy was to concentrate on the Department of State. True, there had been a certain amount of propaganda directed at the public in general through the periodical, *Asia; Journal of the American Asiatic Association*, and true it is also that this propaganda had been meeting with some success. As early as January the *Journal of Commerce*, that close observer of anything pertaining to the Open Door, had pointed to the "new attitude of this country towards its commercial interests in China" and had stated that it was "partly the result of the American Asiatic Association." Nevertheless, greater success had been gained with the State Department. Secretary Sherman and Secretary Day had moved closer to the viewpoint of businessmen who were eager to see the Chinese market safeguarded. John Hay had not once failed to carry out any formal request regarding Far Eastern policy, and, indeed, the department under Hay had shown itself so willing to cooperate that there could be no doubt about its desire to maintain the Open Door in China. . . .

The activity of the special interests during these months of 1899 was of such a nature as to make it extremely difficult to evaluate its significance. It is, of course, quite understandable that no records exist stating explicitly whether or not the administration was influenced by the propaganda campaign, and it is equally understandable that Secretary Hay never wrote down anything which would enable us to judge

whether or not his thinking was affected by the letters from the officials of the Asiatic Association and by the visits these men paid him. It is far easier to trace the effects of the memorials of 1898 than of the propaganda and informal contacts of 1899.

But it would be a great mistake to overlook the possibility that these later activities too were of considerable importance. It may well have been that the *Journal of Commerce* and the Asiatic Association were quite correct in their belief that the propaganda campaign was successful. If it was successful, if it did in fact make the public more conscious of America's stake in the Far East, it doubtless made it easier for the administration to take action designed to preserve the Chinese market. As for the letters and visits from the Asiatic Association to Hay, it is highly probable that such frequent reminders of the desires of certain businessmen had at least the effect of bolstering up the Secretary's own inclinations with respect to China. At any rate, it is clear that these activities of the special interests during the spring and summer of 1899 must have, along with the memorials of 1898, a place in any complete history of the origins of the Open Door policy.

On September 6, 1899, the first group of Open Door notes was dispatched. This was just the kind of step for which the special interests had been hoping and for which they had been working. To the cotton exporters the notes meant that their market appeared to be far more secure; and to the American-China Development Company they meant that there was much to be hoped for from a grateful China—and, indeed, a few months later the company at last secured the contract which it had so long been seeking.

The sending of these notes resulted from a great many factors, one of which was the organized attempt of certain business interests, particularly the men connected with the American China Development Company and the cotton exporters, to persuade the government to take just such a step. It has been shown how these interests, fearful lest the turn of events in China should result in financial loss to themselves, took measures designed to persuade the government to safeguard the Chinese market. First of all, they established the Committee on American Interests in China; later on, when this proved to be too weak an orgaization, they transformed it into the American Asiatic Association. This association, consistently supported by the *Journal of Commerce and Commercial Bulletin*, influential in persuading the administration (and very possibly the general public as well) that a particular line of policy would be of benefit to the nation as a whole. In these facts lies part of the explanation for the formulation of America's Open Door policy.

GEORGE F. KENNAN (1904-   ), a Pulitzer
prize-winning historian, former diplomat, and presently a
member of the Institute for Advanced Study at Princeton
University, argues that the Open Door policy of John Hay
had little substance to it. Because Americans viewed the
Open Door as a considerable achievement, Kennan
believes the policy helped to convince the American people
of their omnipotence. For Kennan, it was an idealistic
policy, one that had an imperfect balance between ends
and means. His assessment of the policy is clearly at odds
with that of Williams. Moreover, Kennan focuses on an
entirely different set of pressures which shaped the policy
from those which Charles S. Campbell, Jr., analyzed. °

An Inadequate Policy

At a time when the European powers
were setting about to partition China and to
appropriate parts of it to their exclusive use,
the American Secretary of State, surmising
their purposes, anticipated them and in
part frustrated their design by sending
them notes which called them to observe in
China the principle of the Open Door—the
principle of equal rights for all, that is—and
of the territorial and administrative integrity of China. The interpretation put
upon this incident by public opinion at the
time and carried down into the textbooks of
our own day is well summed up by Mark
Sullivan in his study entitled *Our Times;*

The "open-door" policy in China was an
American idea. It was set up in contrast to the

"spheres-of-influence" policy practised by
other nations. . . .

The "open-door" is one of the most creditable
episodes in American diplomacy, an example of
benevolent impulse accompanied by energy and
shrewd skill in negotiation. Not one of the
statesmen and nations that agreed to Hay's
policy wanted to. It was like asking every man
who believes in truth to stand up—the liars are
obliged to be the first to rise. Hay saw through
them perfectly; his insight into human nature
was one of his strongest qualities.

Now, bearing in mind this interpretation, let us take a closer look at what really
happened.

At the end of 1897 and the beginning of
1898 there was a real and justifiable fear
that China would be partitioned. It was in

°Reprinted from George F. Kennan, *American Diplomacy, 1900-1950* (Chicago: The University of Chicago
Press, 1951), pp. 21-37. Copyright 1951 by The University of Chicago. Reprinted by permission of the publisher. Footnotes omitted.

those months that the Russians made evident their determination to have a special position in Manchuria, including a naval base at Port Arthur and a commercial port at the present Dairen, both to be connected by railway with the new Trans-Siberian; that the Germans consolidated their control over the port of Kiaochow and their influence in the Shantung Peninsula; and that the French, coming up from the south, from the present Indochina, successfully negotiated with the Chinese government for the lease of a port, for railroad concessions, for the appointment of a French citizen as head of the Chinese postal services, and for other favors.

These happenings naturally caused particular concern in London. Up to that time the British had been the overwhelming masters of the Chinese trade. They had 80 per cent of it; all the rest of the countries together, including ourselves, had only 20 per cent. Being in a favorable competitive position, British traders had always advocated the Open Door in China—that is, equality for everyone in customs treatment, harbor dues, etc., for the importation of consumption merchandise. Now they were not certain how this would all work out with these spheres of influence that other powers were acquiring. Would this operate to exclude British trade or would it not?

This was not a simple question. Up to that time the main difficulties in the China trade had been with the local Chinese authorities in the interior, not with the actions of foreign powers. British merchants had long demanded of their own government that it ignore diplomatic proprieties, ignore the Chinese government in Peking, go right into the interior of China, up the great rivers, with its gunboats, and force the stubborn mandarins to remove the obstructions and exactions which they placed in the path of the movement of merchandise. If this was what the other powers were going

to do in their spheres of influence, perhaps it was a good thing. Perhaps the British could even profit from it. But suppose those powers just opened up the interior to trade and kept it to themselves. Then things would be worse than ever.

The British government, itself, as distinct from the British merchants, had other worries arising out of these events—worries more serious than the complaints and anxieties of British commercial circles. These worries were strategic and political. British statesmen did not like the idea of a Russian naval base on the Gulf of Pechili. Where would all this end? Would it not lead to complete Russian domination of China? The British Foreign Office spoke its fears quite frankly in a secret communication to the czar's government:

A great military Power which is coterminus for over 4,000 miles with the land frontier of China, including the portion lying nearest to its capital, is never likely to be without its due share of influence on the councils of that country. Her Majesty's Government regard it as most unfortunate that it has been thought necessary in addition to obtain control of a port which, if the rest of the Gulf of Pechili remains in hands so helpless as those of the Sovereign Power will command the maritime approaches to its capital, and give to Russia the same strategic advantage by sea which she already possesses in so ample a measure by land.

The Russians paid no attention to this communication and went right ahead with the realization of their plans. After considerable worry and debate the British government responded to this situation in the spring of 1898 in two ways: openly, by stressing the importance of the maintenance of the Open Door in China; covertly, by looking about for some sort of special agreement with some other power or powers for opposing Russia's strategic penetration of Chinese territory. But in the back of their minds they had still a third line of action, a line which they were somewhat reluctant to take at that time but which was being strongly pressed upon them by many of the British merchants in China and which they knew they would have to take if neither of the other methods worked—that was the development of a sphere of influence of their own in the Yangtze Valley, where their own trade was greatest and where they, too, would be able to exert a more direct influence on the government at Peking. By developing such a sphere of influence, they could at least make sure that they would not be excluded from the most important part of China, and there might be other advantages besides.

In the spring of 1898 they still hoped. . . that it would not come to this, but they could not be too sure. Things were changing in China. The Open Door doctrine, the basis of British policy for many years, was beginning to show its limitations generally. In the old days it had been only a question of bringing in consumption goods for general distribution and sale. For such trade the Open Door principle had been clearly applicable and had suited British interests. But now foreign countries were interested in acquiring concessions from the Chinese government for railway construction and mining enterprises. Here, the Open Door principle did not really seem applicable. Such concessions were too important, strategically and politically, for anyone to expect that the Chinese government should be guided only by commercial considerations in granting them. The Chinese government was practically forced to decide in which areas of China it wanted one power to build railways and in which areas another. And there was a good deal to be said for keeping the powers somewhat apart geographically in their concession activities, not all milling around together. If the British wanted to get in on the concession business, which they did, it

was almost essential that they stake out a sphere where their concessions would be concentrated and the concessionaires of other powers excluded.

So there was a deeper logic and necessity behind the growth of these so-called spheres of influence than merely the wickedness of the powers themselves. The Open Door doctrine—a doctrine so old that it was referred to in the British Parliament in 1898 as "that famous phrase that has been quoted and requoted almost *ad nauseam"*—was simply not fully relevant to the new situation. However, the British government thought it still useful to talk about the Open Door and press publicly for its acknowledgment, because trade in consumption goods was still importantly involved, as well as concessions; they did not want to see British merchants excluded anywhere; and, if the principle of commercial "openness" were to be generally respected, this might act as a certain restraint on the expansion of the strategic and political influence of the other powers.

It was against this background that the British government, in March, 1898 (about a month before the outbreak of the Spanish-American War), made its one and only formal approach to the United States government about the Open Door doctrine. It sent a secret communication to President McKinley, pointing out the danger that other powers might annex portions of Chinese territory or lease them under conditions which would assure themselves preferential treatment, and asking "whether they could count on the cooperation of the United States in opposing any such action by Foreign Powers and whether the United States would be prepared to join with Great Britain in opposing such measures should the contingency arise." Please note that they did not come out against spheres of influence. They came out only against annexations or leases of territory under conditions that would exclude the trade of other nations.

There is no evidence that the British Foreign Office attached much importance to this approach or had much hope for its success. The British diplomats were more interested in other overtures they were making about the same time—to Japan and Germany. The approach to us had apparently been pressed upon them by the Colonial Minister, Joseph Chamberlain. Chamberlain, who had an American wife, had high hopes for Anglo-American political co-operation. He was powerful in domestic politics and took a prominent part in the conduct of foreign policy. I suspect that he had been needling the Foreign Office about enlisting American co-operation in China and that the Foreign Office sent the note to our government largely to satisfy him, perhaps even to demonstrate that there was nothing in the idea; but that is only a conjecture.

In any case, nothing came of it at the time. Washington was preoccupied with the Cuban problem. The Department of State did not even have a Far Eastern Division in those days. The Secretary of State, old John Sherman, was inactive, somewhat senile, and about to give over his job. Washington said, in effect, "Nothing doing"; and the matter was not again raised in any formal way by the British government.

. . .one cannot be sure that the British Foreign Office was particularly disappointed with this answer. But there was one man who was. He was John Hay, our ambassador to London. He was absent from London when the approach was made. . . . When he returned and heard what had happened, he sat down and wrote to the Secretary of State asking for a reconsideration of our decision, only to be told that the time was still inopportune.

Hay was presumably interested in the matter exclusively from the standpoint of our relations with England. He knew little if anything about China; he had never been there. But he thought that we were unwise not to be sympathetic to the British in a situation where we might help them and perhaps thereby build up a sort of diplomatic credit on which we could draw later.

In late summer of that year Hay was appointed Secretary of State. Unquestionably, when he came home to assume his duties, he had this matter on his mind. Some of the British had continued to talk to him about it from time to time during the summer, particularly Chamberlain. But, actually, British policy itself was beginning to move quietly away from the Open Door doctrine and continued to do so through the winter of 1898-99. The British statesmen still did lip service to the Open Door principle; but, recognizing that spheres of influence were not to be done away with so easily or to be spurned from the standpoint of their own interests, they proceeded quietly to take certain precautionary measures of their own. To balance the Russian position at Port Arthur, they leased a strategic port on the other side of the Gulf of Pechili. They went into the railway concession business in a big way, particularly in the Yangtze Valley. And they did one more thing which is particularly worth noting in connection with this subject we are discussing today. That was the leasing of Kowloon.

. . .they already had the island of Hongkong as a Crown colony. From there they did business with the mainland of China. I fear that a certain amount of that business may have been irregular in the sense that it evaded payment of the Chinese customs duties; in other words, it was smuggling. Now the Chinese Imperial Maritime Customs Service was at that time an international service administered with great vigor, honesty, and efficiency by an Englishman, Sir Robert Hart. Hart's integrity was such that he did not hesitate to step on the British merchants in China as hard as on anyone else who came into conflict with the customs regulations. Under his uncompromising and rigorous administration the Customs Service, which had acquired some revenue cutters, encircled Hongkong and kept movement between the island and the mainland under strict observation. It was apparently partly as a counter to this that the British, in June, 1898, acquired a lease on a portion of the Chinese mainland across the strait from Hongkong—the piece of territory known as Kowloon. With Kowloon in their possession it would be possible for goods to pass from Hongkong to the mainland without customs supervision. And it is significant that one of their first acts after acquiring the territory was to close the customhouse of the Chinese Imperial Maritime Customs. This was naturally a source of concern to Sir Robert Hart and the Customs Service. With the Germans and the Russians, they had thus far had no trouble. The Germans had even invited them to set up a customhouse in their port of Kiaochow, where there had not been one before. But Hart was very apprehensive about what the Russians might do in the future. If the British were going to set this sort of a precedent, by expelling the Customs Service from Kowloon, and if the precedent were followed by others, then the establishment of the spheres of influence might conceivably lead to the closing of customhouses everywhere in the so-called spheres of influence, to the complete breakup of the Customs Service itself, and to the financial ruin of the Chinese government.

When John Hay took up his duties as Secretary of State in the late months of 1898, he had no adviser on Far Eastern affairs. He therefore brought back to Washington a friend of his, W. W. Rockhill.

Rockhill was then minister to Greece. He had served in China before, but it was seven years since he had been there, and he was somewhat out of touch with conditions. . . .we may at least suppose that what Hay wanted him to do was to find some way of responding to the British request that we help them in their China problem.

Rockhill got back in the spring of 1899 but apparently was not immediately able to recommend any action along this line. There is some evidence that the President was still averse to taking any such action. In his message to Congress, in December, 1898, he had spoken as though the problem were one which had largely solved itself. We are also justified in suspecting that Rockhill himself did not know just how to tackle the problem—what action to take. The British were not renewing their request about the Open Door; they showed very little interest in it, as a matter of fact. The British ambassador, following the good old custom of that day, went away to Newport for the summer and was not available for consultation. Actually. . .the British government was slipping rapidly away from the Open Door policy in their actions in China and probably had no desire at that time to be reminded of it.

Then events began to happen. In the middle of June there arrived in the Washington area an old friend of Rockhill's from Peking: an Englishman by the name of Hippisley, who was second in command of the Chinese Customs Service, under Sir Robert Hart. Hippisley was on leave of absence from his post in China and was passing through the United States on his way to England. His wife was a Baltimore girl and a friend of Mrs. Rockhill. Presumably still smarting under the effect of the British action at Kowloon, and imbued with the necessity of preserving the authority of the Imperial Maritime Customs Service over the importation of goods into China, he urged that the American government "do what it can to maintain the Open Door for ordinary commerce in China." Spheres of interest, he said, were there to stay and had to be treated as existing facts. So long as they were taken to apply only to railroad and mining concessions, it was all right. But if people began to extend this concept to customs treatment, dangers would arise. With this in view he urged that the United States approach the other European powers and get from each of them an assurance that they would not interfere with treaty ports in their spheres of influence (that is, with ports where the Imperial Maritime Customs Service had its establishments) and that the Chinese treaty tariff should apply without discrimination to all merchandise entering their respective spheres of influence.

Rockhill was taken with these ideas. But at first he thought they were unfeasible from the domestic political standpoint. So did Hay. . . . "I am fully awake to the great importance of what you say," Hay wrote to Rockhill on August 7, "and am more than ready to act. But the senseless prejudices in certain sections of the 'Senate and people' compel us to move with great caution."

Shortly after this, however, things suddenly changed. For one reason or another the domestic political inhibitions to taking action seem to have been overcome. On August 24, Hay gave Rockhill authorization to go ahead with Hippisley's suggestion. Basing his position largely on a memorandum drafted by Hippisley, Rockhill drew up a paper which was presented to the President and approved by him. On the basis of this paper, in turn, a series of notes were drawn up, addressed to the various powers which had interests in China. . . .

The notes began with a discussion of the background. This discussion embodied some of Hippisley's thoughts but also included some of Rockhill's own ideas. It contained a refusal by the United States government to recognize the spheres of influence at all, whereas Hippisley had said they were there to stay and that there was no use challenging them. But the kernel of the notes lay in a concrete three-point formula, quite technical in working, which was taken almost verbatim from Hipisley's memorandum. There is no evidence that this formula was given any serious critical study in the United States government or that any effort was made to assess the practical significance it would have when measured against events in China. It seems to me likely, in view of its origin and wording, that it was a carefully prepared summary of the desires of the Chinese Imperial Maritime Customs Service at that particular moment. It also seems likely that it was really aimed largely at the British. By getting our government to sponsor it, Hippisley had obviously found a convenient roundabout way of putting pressure on the British government to behave in a manner less threatening to the interests of the Customs Service in China. But there is no indication that either Rockhill or John Hay was aware of this aspect of the matter or had any idea of the extent to which Hippisley's formula might be in conflict with British policy at that particular moment. That they suspected the British of sideslipping a bit from the straight-and-narrow path of the Open Door seems probable. I would doubt, however, that they understood how far this deviation had gone and how little agreeable to the British would be the formula contained in the notes.

The reception given to the notes by the various governments was tepid, to say the least. The British failed to register enthusiasm, bickered for a long time about the application of the formula to Kowloon, and finally gave a conditional assent—that is, they would subscribe to our principles to the extent that everybody else might subscribe to them. Since everybody else made the same condition, the replies were no stronger than their weakest link. The weakest link was obviously Russia. The language of the Russian reply was cryptic and evasive. Our ambassador at St. Petersburg warned Hay that the Russian government "did not wish to answer your propositions at all. It did so finally with great reluctance." Despite this warning—so reminiscent of many warnings which were later to be given by the American Embassy in Moscow against placing too much faith in verbal assurances wormed out of the Soviet government—Hay did not hesitate to announce on March 20,1900, that he had received satisfactory assurances from all the powers and that he regarded them as "final and definitive." He thereby gave the impression, which the American public was not slow to accept, that the European powers, who had been on the verge of getting away with something improper in China, had been checked and frustrated by the timely intervention of the United States government and that a resounding diplomatic triumph had been achieved.

In doing this . . .he created a precedent which was destined to bedevil American diplomatic practice for at least a half-century thereafter and may—as far as I can see—continue to bedevil it for another half-century still. . .

This was not all that there was to the story of the Open Door notes. There was an epilogue. Hay's announcement that he had received satisfactory assurances from the foreign powers about the Open Door principle happened to coincide almost exactly with the beginning of the Boxer Rebellion. This was. . .a violent and fanatical anti-foreign movement, in part connived at by the Chinese government, which led to much destruction of foreign property, to the killing of a number of foreigners, to the

flight of thousands more from the interior, and to a full-fledged military attack on the foreign legations in Peking, who were surrounded and besieged and forced to defend themselves with arms over a period of several weeks, until relieving expeditions reached the city.

It was a presidential election year in the United States. The siege of the legations in Peking began on June 20 and ended on August 14. The Republican National Convention met in Philadelphia on June 19 and the Democratic Convention in Kansas City on July 4. The air was already ringing with controversies about "imperialism," which grew out of the decisions surrounding the Spanish-American War. The administration felt no desire to be drawn any more deeply than necessary into military ventures in China or to be harassed that summer by any further explosive issues of foreign policy. On July 3, one day before the opening of the Democratic National Convention, Hay issued to the powers another circular, this time defining—in what were apparently intended to be soothing and noncontroversial terms— American policy toward China in the light of the existing disorder and anarchy in that country. In the first Open Door notes he had mentioned the desirability of maintaining the integrity of China but had not stressed this point. Now, in the circular of July 3, 1900, it was specifically stated that "the policy of the Government of the United States is to seek. . .to preserve Chinese territorial and administrative entity." This reference to the territorial and administrative "entity" of China has been taken by historians as adding a new note to the thoughts put forward in the original Open Door communications and as committing this government to the protection of China against foreign encroachments on her territory. That was indeed to be the interpretation put upon it and followed by the United States government for most of the next fifty years. The Open Door notes are thus generally considered to have been those addressed to the powers in the summer of 1899 plus the circular issued during the Boxer Rebellion in the following summer.

Actually, none of these communications had any perceptible practical effect. The later circular, in fact, was scarcely noticed at all outside our own country. There was little reason to expect that things would be otherwise. The Boxer Rebellion, accompanied as it was by foreign military intervention, was bound to lead to a net increase, rather than decrease, in the authority exerted by foreign governments in China. The Russians used it to strengthen their hold on Manchuria. And the indemnities levied against the Chinese government forced the latter to increase its borrowings from one or the other of the powers, and hence its dependence on them.

The authors of the American Open Door policy soon became themselves quite disillusioned with it. It seemed to be almost swallowed up in the march of events. To Hippisley, the Boxer Rebellion meant the inevitable breakup of China, which in turn meant the end of the Open Door. Rockhill, who was sent out to Peking as a special United States commissioner to help reorganize Chinese affairs after the rebellion, is said to have written, only two years after the first Open Door notes were sent: "I trust it may be a long time before the United States gets into another muddle of this description."

As for Hay himself, in December, 1900, only five months after his proclamation of devotion to the principle of upholding Chinese territorial and administrative "entity," he secretly instructed our minister in Peking to try to obtain for the United States a naval coaling station at Samsah Bay in the Chinese province of Fukien. But when, a few weeks later, the Japanese, alarmed by the increasing pace of Russian encroachment in Manchuria, inquired politely whether the United States would be inclined to join them in using force to assure the observance of the principles it had enunciated, Hay replied that the United States was "not at present prepared to attempt singly, or in concert with other Powers, to enforce these views in the east by any demonstration which could present a character of hostility to any other Power."

There is every reason to believe that the Japanese took the most careful and attentive note of the significance of this statement. They were interested then, as always, in real military allies, not halfhearted ones. One year later they signed the Anglo-Japanese alliance on which their security was to be based for many years to come. Three years later they took up arms and threw the Russians out of the south of Manchuria. In doing these things, they neither expected our aid nor feared our opposition. Had not Hay said that our views about China were not ones which we would enforce by any demonstration which could present a character of hostility to any other power?

These, then, were the circumstances surrounding the issuance of John Hay's Open Door notes. When you analyze them, what did they amount to? It seems to me that they amounted to something like this.

In the summer of 1899 the American Secretary of State approached a number of other powers and asked them to subscribe to a certain formula designed to govern the policies of countries that had acquired spheres of influence in China.

It was not a formula which Hay had drafted. There is no evidence that he understood fully its practical significance. One of his assistants had bought it sight unseen, so to speak, from an Englishman who had happened to be in the vicinity of Washington that summer. It was probably thought to be responsive to a request the British had made of us. Actually, it did not represent English policy of the moment; it was even somewhat in conflict with that policy. It may have represented the aspirations of the Chinese Imperial Maritime Customs Service in the face of certain developments which threatened its future. It was not a new policy but an old one. It was not an American policy but one long established in British relations with China. It was not a policy that in general had a future; it was an antiquated one, already partially overtaken by developments. It was not a policy that we Americans cared enough about to support in any determined way or for the results of which, if implemented, we were prepared to accept any particular responsibility. Finally, as events were shortly to show, it was not even a policy to which we ourselves would be inclined to adhere in our own possessions, for within a few years after our acquisition of the Philippines and Puerto Rico—and despite our brave promises to the contrary—we set up discriminatory regimes, conflicting with the Open Door principle, in both of these newly acquired territories.

There is no evidence that Hay was aware of these realities, in so far as they were the realities of the moment, or was capable of foreseeing them, in so far as they pertained to the future. There is perhaps no reason to suppose that he should have. The formula had a high-minded and idealistic ring; it would sound well at home; it was obviously in the interests of American trade; the British had been known to advocate it—still did, so far as he knew—and it was hard to see what harm could come from trying it on the other powers. This he did. He got the grudging, embarrassed, and evasive replies which might have been expected. He was warned of the lack of substance in these replies, but he saw no reason why he should not turn to the American public and make the best of it by representing these answers as a diplomatic success.

For all this, I do not blame him and do not mean to censure him. He was a man of his time—a man of dignity and sensitivity—a great American gentlemen. He labored in a framework of government which was unsuited, really, to the conduct of the foreign affairs of a great power. He was making the best of an unsatisfactory situation.

But what I do want to stress, and this is the central point of this discussion, is that the American public found no difficulty in accepting this action as a major diplomatic achievement. Its imagination was fired, its admiration won. Hay was established in its affections as a great statesman. The popularity of the administration's foreign policy was materially improved just at the time of the coming presidential elections.

Not only was this effect achieved at the moment, but a myth was established which was destined to flourish in American thinking for at least a half-century. Neither the obvious lack of practical results, nor the disillusionment of Hay and the other persons involved, nor our unwillingness to bolster the policy in any forceful way, nor our subsequent departure from it ourselves—none of these things succeeded in shaking in any way the established opinion of the American public that here, in this episode of the Open Door notes, a tremendous blow had been struck for the triumph of American principles in international society—an American blow for an American idea.

Suggestions for Further Reading

Few subjects of American history have a literature more vast than that which bears on American expansionism. One may approach the subject from the vantage point of local history or from that of world diplomacy. For example, one may study the attitudes and actions of various groups in American communities toward expansionism or focus on the response of political leaders either to domestic pressures at various levels of society or to foreign events. Because American expansionism involves forces that range from being local to worldwide in character, the student who wishes to read further on the subject has an almost unlimited choice of where he may begin.

The best book for placing American expansionism of the 1890s in its world setting is William L. Langer, *The Diplomacy of Imperialism* (New York, 1951). For a study of the reaction of various European states to American diplomacy of the 1890s, see Ernest R. May, *Imperial Democracy: The Emergence of America as a Great Power* (New York, 1961); indeed, this is one of the few books on American foreign policy during this period which concentrates on the intricate relations between the United States and various European governments. In "American Imperialism: A Reinterpretation," *Perspectives in American History*, I (1967), 123-283, May has written a provocative essay that assesses the impact of English and European ideas on American opinion.

A book of perceptive essays which amount to a general treatment of American foreign policy in the late nineteenth century is John A. S. Grenville and George B. Young, *Politics, Strategy, and American Diplomacy* (New Haven, Conn., 1966). But the best detailed study of American diplomacy of the early 1880s is David M.

Pletcher, *The Awkward Years: American Foreign Relations Under Garfield and Arthur* (Columbia, Mo., 1962). This book is especially useful not only because it is thorough but because it focuses on a period of American diplomacy that seldom receives the attention it deserves.

Unusually thoughtful and provocative analyses of the ideas behind American expansion are: Frederick Merk, *Manifest Destiny and Mission in American History* (New York, 1963); Albert Weinberg, *Manifest Destiny* (Baltimore, Md., 1935); and William A. Williams, *The Contours of American History* (Cleveland, Ohio, 1961). Each of these books is a distinctive work of historical scholarship, none of which overlaps or duplicates the other in any meaningful way. Every serious student of American expansionism should read each of them.

There are numerous studies that assess the impact of various groups on certain aspects of American expansionism. For the relationship between businessmen and expansionism during the 1890s, see Charles S. Campbell, Jr., *Special Business Interests and the Open Door Policy* (New Haven, Conn., 1951); Julius W. Pratt, *Expansionists of 1898* (Baltimore, Md., 1938); and Walter LaFeber, *The New Empire: An Interpretation of American Expansion, 1860-1898* (Ithaca, N.Y., 1963). The role various governmental agencies played in shaping American expansionism is still unclear, but several studies that focus, in very different ways, on the navy's influence are: Harold and Margaret Sprout, *The Rise of American Naval Power* (Princeton, N.J. 1939); Robert Seager, "Ten Years Before Mahan: The Unofficial Case for the New Navy, 1880-1890," *Mississippi Valley Historical Review*, XL (December, 1953), 491-518; and

William R. Braisted, *The United States Navy in the Pacific* (Austin, 1958).

American diplomatic historians have frequently written more about the impact of public opinion on policy than on the actual shaping of policy. In this respect, several studies that analyze public opinon as reflected in newspapers are: George W. Auxier, "Middle Western Newspapers and the Spanish American War, 1895-1898," *Mississippi Valley Historical Review*, XXVI (March, 1940), 523-534. Marcus M. Wilkerson, *Public Opinion and the Spanish-American War: A Study in War Propaganda* (Baton Rouge, 1932); and Joseph E. Wisan, *The Cuban Crisis as Reflected in the New York Press, 1895-1898* (New York, 1934). Unfortunately, these studies reveal very little about the influence of public opinion on the actual process of policy making. Regrettably, the process of decision making is a subject of American diplomacy about which we are still poorly informed.

There were many different kinds of expansionism, and the literature for each is vast. For example, there is an immense literature on the efforts to acquire an extraterritorial empire. In this respect, a useful essay is George W. Baker, "Benjamin Harrison and Hawaiian Annexation: A Reinterpretation," *Pacific Historical Review*, XXXIII (August, 1964), 295-309. The best studies focusing on the debate over annexation of the Philippines are: W. Stull Holt, *Treaties Defeated by the Senate* (Baltimore, Md., 1933); Fred H. Harrington, "The Anti-Imperialist Movement in the United States, 1898-1900," *Mississippi Valley Historical Review*, XXII (September, 1935), 211-230; and Richard Hofstadter, "Manifest Destiny and the Philippines," in Daniel Aaron (ed.), *America in Crisis* (New York, 1952), pp. 173-200. A study in domestic politics, J. Rogers Hollingsworth, *The Whirligig of Politics: The Democracy of Cleveland and Bryan* (Chicago, Ill., 1963), assesses the role of various Democrats in promoting different kinds of expansionism.

There are many studies on the origins of the Spanish-American War, and as with most complex events, there is lack of agreement among historians concerning the significance of various contributing factors. Even so, the two most useful books are: Walter LaFeber, *The New Empire: An Interpretation of American Expansion*, which emphasizes economic forces as moving McKinley toward war, and Julius W. Pratt, *Expansionists of 1898*, which tends to minimize economic considerations. For the war itself, Walter Millis, *The Martial Spirit* (New York, 1931) is a very readable study written from the anti-imperialist point of view by an author who finds it difficult to be serious about the war. The best brief summary of the war, as well as of the immediate problems arising from it, is H. Wayne Morgan, *America's Road to Empire: The War with Spain and Overseas Expansion* (New York, 1965). A most enjoyable book is Frank Freidel, *The Splendid Little War* (Boston, 1958), containing the works of many of the participants as well as numerous photographs of the war.

Two assessments of 1898 as a turning point in American foreign policy are: Norman A. Graebner, "The Year of Transition—1898," in Norman A. Graebner (ed.), *An Uncertain Tradition: American Secretaries of State in the Twentieth Century* (New York, 1961) and Thomas A. Bailey, "America's Emergence as a World Power: The Myth and the Verity," *Pacific Historical Review*, XXX (February, 1961), 1-16. Though these essays reach somewhat opposite conclusions, each is highly recommended reading for all students of American foreign policy.

During the past decade, a number of excellent studies have focused on American economic expansionism. Even so, our understanding of this subject is still inadequate. A penetrating study that places one aspect of economic expansionism within its international context is Morton Rothstein, "America in the International Rivalry for the British Wheat Market, 1860-1914," *Mississippi Valley Historical Review*, XLVII (December, 1960), 401-418. The relationship between the demand for lower tariffs and the search for foreign markets is an important subject about which there has been little published. But an important unpublished study is Tom E. Terrill, "The Tariff and American Foreign Policy, 1880-1892" (Ph.D. dissertation, University of Wisconsin, 1966). Other useful studies focusing on the relationship between tariffs and the search for foreign markets are: Bingham Duncan, "Protectionism and Park: Whitelaw Reid as Diplomat, 1889-1891," *Agricultural History*, XXXIII (December, 1959), 190-195, and John Gignillat, "Pigs, Politics and Protection: The European Boycott of American Park, 1879-1891," *Agricultural History*, XXXV (January, 1961), 3-12.

For literature which suggests that the Open Door policy provided a solution to the debate over imperialism, see the perceptive studies by Thomas J. McCormick: "A Commentary on the Anti-Imperialists and Twentieth-Century Foreign Policy," *Studies on the Left*, III (1962), 28-33, and "'A Fair Field and No Favor': American China Policy during the McKinley Administrations, 1897-1901" (Ph.D. dissertation, University of Wisconsin, 1960). Paul A. Varg, *Open Door Diplomat: The Life of W. W. Rockhill* (Urbana, Ill., 1952) does a great deal to clarify previously disputed points about the origins of the Open Door policy. Though parts of Tyler Dennett, *Americans in Eastern Asia* (New York, 1922) have been superseded, this is still the best general account of American relations with the Far East during the nineteenth century. A. Whitney Griswold, *The Far Eastern Policy of the United States* (New York, 1938) is a general survey of American diplomatic relations with the Far East relying primarily on American official documents.

The best studies of secretaries of state during this period are: Chester L. Barrows, *William M. Evarts* (Chapel Hill, N.C., 1941); Charles C. Tansill, *The Foreign Policy of Thomas F. Bayard, 1885-1897* (New York, 1940); and Alice Felt Tyler, *The Foreign Policy of James G. Blaine* (Minneapolis, Minn., 1927). Tyler Dennett's highly readable Pulitzer prize-winning study, *John Hay: From Poetry to Politics* (New York, 1934) is an outstanding biography, though a bit too favorable to Hay. Unfortunately, there are no thorough studies of Frederick Frelinghuysen, Walter Gresham, Richard Olney, and John Sherman. There are, however, very useful brief essays on these men in Samuel F. Bemis (ed.), *American Secretaries of State and Their Diplomacy* (10 vols.; New York, 1927-1929).

One of the best presidential biographies containing material on American expansionism is Allan Nevins, *Grover Cleveland: A Study in Courage* (New York, 1947). Margaret Leech, *In the Days of McKinley* (New York, 1959), H.

Wayne Morgan, *William McKinley and His America* (Syracuse, N.Y., 1963), and Paul S. Holbo, "Presidential Leadership in Foreign Affairs: William McKinley and the Turpie-Foraker Amendment," *American Historical Review*, LXXII (July, 1967), 1321-1335, do much to correct earlier views that McKinley was a weak president with few foreign policies of his own. There is no full-length study of Harrison, but A. T. Volwiler, "Harrison, Blaine, and Foreign Policy, 1889-1893," *American Philosophical Society Proceedings*, LXXIX (1938), 637-648, is a good introduction to the diplomacy of his administration.

For the late nineteenth century, there are biographies of numerous other public officials. Among the most useful studies of a Republican leader is John Garraty, *Henry Cabot Lodge* (New York, 1953). Also important for understanding various phases of expansionism is Elmer Ellis, *Henry Moore Teller* (Caldwell, Idaho, 1941), a study of an influential Silver Republican from Colorado. John R. Lambert, *Arthur P. Gorman* (Baton Rouge, 1953) and Festus P. Summers, *William L. Wilson and Tariff Reform* (New Brunswick, N.J., 1953) are good studies of two influential Democrats who usually disagreed over the means of promoting economic expansionism.

There were a number of individuals outside of government who exerted considerable influence on American expansionism and for whom we have good studies. A useful work focusing on Bryan's activities is Merle Curti, *Bryan and World Peace* ("Smith College Studies in History," XVI [Northampton, Mass., 1931]). For studies of individuals who did much to publicize the necessity for expanding foreign markets, see Harold Francis Williamson, *Edward Atkinson: The Biography of an American Liberal* (Boston, 1934); Fred B. Joyner, *David Ames Wells, Champion of Free Trade* (Cedar Rapids, Iowa, 1939); William A. Williams, "Brooks Adams and American Expansion," *New England Quarterly*, XXV (June, 1952), 217-232. and Charles Vevier, "Brooks Adams and the Ambivalence of American Foreign Policy," *World Affairs Quarterly*, XXX (April, 1959), 3-18.

There are numerous studies which focus on the relations between the United States and other countries and which contain important information about specific aspects of expansionism. American economic expansionism is explored in Fred Harvey Harrington, *God, Mammon, and the Japanese: Dr. Horace N. Allen and Korean-American Relations, 1884-1905* (Madison, 1944). An excellent study of the formative years of American policy in Cuba is David F. Healy, *The United States in Cuba, 1898-1902* (Madison, 1963). For early economic penetration into Mexico, an important study is David M. Pletcher, *Rails, Mines, and Progress: Seven American Promoters in Mexico, 1867-* *1911* (Ithaca, N.Y. 1958). The best treatment of the Monroe Doctrine and its relationship to American expansionism for these years is Dexter Perkins, *The Monroe Doctrine, 1867-1907* (Baltimore, Md., 1937). For global aspects of American expansionism as it affected England, see Charles S. Campbell, Jr., *Anglo-American Understanding, 1898-1903* (Baltimore, Md., 1957).

There are many other studies about American expansionism which are useful, and a careful examination of the bibliographies in the above mentioned books should offer suggestions for further reading.